OSPREY MILITARY CAMPAIGN SERIES: 56

EGGMÜHL 1809

STORM OVER BAVARIA

SERIES EDITOR: LEE JOHNSON

OSPREY MILITARY CAMPAIGN SERIES: 56

EGGMÜHL 1809

STORM OVER BAVARIA

TEXT BY
IAN CASTLE

BATTLESCENES BY
CHRISTA HOOK

First published in Great Britain in 1998 by Osprey Publishing
Elms Court, Chapel Way, Botley, Oxford OX2 9LP United Kingdom

ISBN 1 85532 708 2

Military Editor: Nikolai Bogdanovic
Design: The Black Spot

Colour bird's eye view illustrations by Trevor Lawrence
Cartography by Mioromap
Wargaming Eggmühl by Ian Dickie
Battlescene artwork by Christa Hook
Filmset in Great Britain by Valhaven Ltd.
Printed through World Print Ltd., Hong Kong

98 99 00 01 02   10 9 8 7 6 5 4 3 2 1

For a catalogue of all books published by Osprey Military please write to:

The Marketing Manager, Osprey Publishing Ltd., PO Box 140, Wellingborough, Northants NN8 4ZA United Kingdom.

Key to military symbols

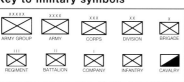

Acknowledgements

Most earlier works covering the 1809 campaign have relied heavily on French sources alone. I have been fortunate enough to have consulted the excellent Austrian Staff history *Krieg 1809*, gaining a more balanced view of this campaign. I owe a great debt of gratitude to David Hollins for his excellent translation of this work and his continued encouragement and assistance.

In addition, I would like to thank David Wright, Philipp Elliot-Wright, Martin Wörel, Philip Haythornthwaite, Grant Elliot and John Henderson for their generous help.

Photo Acknowledgements

ASKB = Anne S.K. Brown Military Collection
ÖNB = Österreichische NationalBibliotek
Bayerische Verwaltung = Bayerische Verwaltung der staatl, Schlösser, Garten und Seen, Museumabteilung, Munich
Unless otherwise stated all illustrations are from the author's collection.

Publisher's Note

Readers may wish to study this title in conjunction with the following Osprey publications:

MAA 55 *Napoleon's Dragoons and Lancers*
MAA 64 *Napoleon's Cuirassiers & Carabiniers*
MAA 68 *Napoleon's Line Chasseurs*
MAA 76 *Napoleon's Hussars*
MAA 83 *Napoleon's Guard Cavalry*
MAA 87 *Napoleon's Marshals*
MAA 146 *Napoleon's Light Infantry*
MAA 176 *Austrian Army of the Napoleonic Wars (1) Infantry*
MAA 181 *Austrian Army of the Napoleonic Wars (2) Cavalry*
MAA 199 *Napoleon's Specialist Troops*
MAA 223 *Austrian Specialist Troops of the Napoleonic Wars*
MAA 299 *Austrian Auxiliary Troops 1792-1816*
Campaign 25 *Leipzig 1813*
Campaign 33 *Aspern and Wagram 1809*
Warrior 22 *Imperial Guardsman 1799-1815*
Warrior 24 *Austrian Grenadiers and Infantry 1788-1816*

Author's Note

This volume, detailing the early part of the campaign between Austria and France in 1809, follows an earlier work in this series (Campaign 33: *Aspern & Wagram 1809*) which highlighted the two climactic battles at the end of the campaign. To avoid repetition of the background to the campaign, given in the early sections of the previous title, in the initial section of this work I have concentrated more on changes and developments in the armies and commanders following France's defeat of Austria in 1805. In addition it appears unnecessary to repeat the chronology of the campaign and the guide to further reading given in the earlier work, and I recommend that this volume be read in conjunction with Campaign 33.

PAGE 2 **The Battle of Alteglofsheim.**

CONTENTS

THE ROAD TO WAR, 1809

Emperor Francis I (Kaiser Franz) of Austria (1768-1835). Francis succeeded his father, Leopold II, in 1792, on the eve of the outbreak of the Revolutionary Wars. The first 23 years of his reign were dominated by the wars against France, and later Napoleon.

LEFT The campaign of 1809 was to prove a great test for Napoleon. He entered the arena late, being stung into action by Archduke Charles' early advance into Bavaria. He had a low opinion of the Austian army at this time and allowed it to cloud his overview as the counter-offensive developed. Ultimately it was only his great ability to rapidly redeploy that ensured a successful opening to the campaign. (ASKB)

"For the present nothing more is to be hoped than they may have made a safe and effectual retreat." So wrote the British ambassador in Vienna upon hearing the news of the defeat of the Russo-Austrian army at Austerlitz in December 1805. It had been a disastrous campaign for Austria, and the humiliating surrender of an army of 25,000 men at Ulm in October followed by this further defeat in Moravia brought the campaign to an end. With the Russians retreating eastwards, all that was left for Austria was to sue for peace and hope to emerge from the resultant talks without having to pay too high a price. The Treaty of Pressburg, signed later in December, destroyed this hope. In addition to a large financial indemnity, Austria lost great tracts of land, much of it being ceded to the fledgling Kingdom of Italy, with Napoleon recognised as its king. Other lands were handed to Napoleon's ally Bavaria, and Austria was forced to accept Bavaria and Württemberg as independent kingdoms, freed from ties to the Habsburg-ruled Holy Roman Empire. This removal of Austria's influence in Germany led to the dissolution of the Holy Roman Empire, and in its place the Confederation of the Rhine (Rheinbund) was created, owing its loyalty and manpower to France. The stark severity of this settlement was to ensure that Austria would rise again and don once more the mantle of war.

The call to arms came when a joint French–Spanish force marched into Portugal in November 1807. This move was the opening act in a drama that was to run for eight years and draw tens of thousands of Napoleon's best soldiers away from central Europe to be consumed in the crucible that later became known as the Peninsular War. However, the following year relations between the two allies deteriorated, and soon France was at war with Spain too. Initial French success was halted by the surrender of a corps at Bailen in July 1808. A month later the French were defeated at Vimiero by an Anglo-Portuguese army commanded by Sir Arthur Wellesley, forcing the French to abandon Portugal.

The myth of French invincibility had been broken; in Europe all eyes were focused on Spain. Aware of the pressing need for his presence with the army, Napoleon met with Tsar Alexander of Russia. Having secured assurances that Russia would oppose any aggressive action by Austria in central Europe, Napoleon prepared to leave for Spain. Orders were issued for the transferral of about 100,000 of his best soldiers from Germany. At the same time, in Vienna's corridors of power, those who supported a return to war were in the ascendancy. In the spring of 1809 they would have their way; the Russians, observing developments, merely offered a token gesture of opposition.

On 23 December 1808 the decision to go to war was taken. It was to be an offensive operation "beyond the borders of the frontier" (Archduke Charles). It would be necessary to inflict a major defeat on French forces, and to this end Germany was the obvious target since, despite the exodus to Spain, large numbers of French and Allied troops were still based there. Charles favoured a major advance from Bohemia north of the Danube, with a smaller supporting force operating south of the river. In addition, secondary operations were to be ordered in northern Italy, the Tyrol, Poland and Dalmatia. On 16 February 1809 the order was issued for the army to begin to concentrate in the 11 newly created army korps. By late February six korps were positioned in Bohemia (I, II, III, IV, V and I Reserve), while south of the Danube two korps lay on the Inn river (VI and II Reserve). Meanwhile, on the secondary fronts two korps (VIII and IX) were preparing to move into Italy, while far away to the east VII Korps in Galicia were ready to advance on Warsaw.

Archduke Charles and his staff in 1809. 1 Charles. 2 Liechtenstein (I Reserve Korps). 3 Hiller (VI Korps). 4 Bellegarde (I Korps). 5 Hohenzollern (III Korps). 6 Rosenberg (IV Korps).

OPPOSING ARMIES

ARCHDUKE CHARLES
AND THE AUSTRIAN ARMY

At the beginning of the 19th century the Austrian court was, as it had always been, a place of great intrigue. The military hierarchy was no exception, as differing factions vied for the ear of the emperor and control of the army. Following Austria's defeat by France in 1800, Archduke Charles (Erzherzog Karl) had risen to a position of power and planned to instigate both military and civil reforms. There were a number who opposed him, and even his own brother, Emperor Francis II, was suspicious of his intentions. Charles was criticised for investing too much time and money in administrative reforms and not enough in preparing the army for a renewal of war.

As the possibility of a new war against France developed through 1804 and into 1805, Charles advocated that the army was not ready for a return to conflict. Armed with this ammunition, Charles' rivals pushed forward Feldmarschalleutnant Mack as their champion. Charles' power was cut away as Mack's influence grew, until it was clear that Mack had gained the ascendancy. When the campaign of 1805 opened, Mack was in command of the army in Germany, thrusting boldly westwards, far ahead of his Russian allies. At the same time, Charles was advancing into northern Italy with another army, convinced of Mack's impending defeat. Charles' fears were confirmed in October 1805, when his rival was forced to surrender his army at Ulm. The victorious French rolled on eastwards and defeated a combined Russo-Austrian army at Austerlitz; the war was over. Charles emerged from the campaign with his reputation intact, and when Austria began to reorganise her army once more in the aftermath of Austerlitz, Charles was appointed overall commander, early in 1806. He immediately placed his supporters in positions of power and removed those openly opposed to him. This did little to ease his brother's suspicions.

As Charles began his work, news came of Prussia's intentions of reopening war with Napoleon. Despite mounting pressure, Charles resisted all attempts to persuade Austria to join the new Prussian–Russian coalition. Unconvinced that the time was right or that the allies could succeed, Charles successfully steered Austria away from the

Archduke Charles (Erzherzog Karl), 1771-1847. Charles was Francis' younger brother and first saw military service in 1793. In 1796 he commanded the Army of the Rhine. Over the next few years his military fortunes fluctuated, until in 1806 he was given complete control of the Austrian army after the disastrous Ulm/Austerlitz campaign.

conflict that threatened. Despite the subsequent defeat of the Prussians at Jena-Auerstädt, the pressure continued against Charles, and it increased following the Battle of Eylau, in which a Russo-Prussian force had checked Napoleon. Again Charles refused to alter his stance. The war finally came to an end following the French victory over the Russians at Friedland in 1807. Charles continued his work, but was constantly hampered by the intrigues against him; even the emperor asked for secret reports from Charles' own supporters to help him restrict his brother's power.

During this period of reform and reorganisation Charles collaborated on the production of a book, which was published under his name, entitled *The Fundamentals of the Higher Art of War for the Generals of the Austrian Army*. The book outlined Charles' ideas on strategy, generalship, grand tactics and the nature of war. Although still largely late 18th century in its outlook, the book showed that he had learned from his recent experiences in fighting against the French. However, it did little to encourage initiative among the senior generals, who with an average age of 63 were probably a little too set in their ways to absorb any new ideas with enthusiasm. Turning his attention to the regimental officers, Charles issued a series of manuals which offered insight into his thinking on such subjects as the use of advance guards, reconnaissance, skirmishing, attacking and defending woods, villages and field fortifications.

In 1807 Charles had worked on a new set of regulations for the infantry, which he believed streamlined general procedures, although some of the innovations officially introduced at this time had been in practice since 1805. Infantry regiments were returned to a strength of two grenadier companies and three battalions, each of six companies. Eight Jäger battalions were created and, although initially opposed to the idea, Charles eventually accepted the need for the raising of a Landwehr. The cavalry had received new regulations in 1806, although these mainly confirmed changes which had occurred in 1804. Also in 1807, Charles made improvements in the lives of the soldiers of the army. By condemning the imposition of harsh discipline and encouraging an esprit de corps in the regiments, he improved morale, and by introducing shorter periods of service in the ranks, he made the army a slightly more attractive proposition. This had the added benefit of building up a trained army reserve.

There were flaws in Charles' plans for the army: he had hoped to improve its manoeuvrability and flexibility by following the French principle of forming independent corps, but lack of funds in the treasury had made it impossible to bring the army together for training prior to the onset of war. So although the army entered the war of 1809 in the new corps formations, the senior officers had little practical knowledge of independent command and had no experience in exercising individual initiative.

As the threat of this new war with France loomed during 1808, tensions grew in Austria. Even Charles accepted that a renewal of war against Napoleon, now deeply embroiled in Spain, was imminent. But with the army once more placed on a war-footing, Charles' old doubts returned, and again he expressed the view that the army was not ready for a return to conflict. Despite his doubts, Charles was confirmed by Emperor Francis as supreme military commander, and as such launched the attack into Bavaria in April 1809.

NAPOLEON AND THE FRENCH-ALLIED ARMY

The year of 1805 had seen Napoleon fight and win his first campaign as emperor of France. In a few short weeks he had led his newly styled Grande Armée across central Europe, crushing the armies of Austria and Russia in the process. The peace talks that followed had punished Austria severely for its part in the war. In addition it had opened the way for Napoleon to dismember the ancient Holy Roman Empire and in its place authorise the creation of the Confederation of the Rhine (Rheinbund). This was exactly what Napoleon had hoped for: a buffer zone of friendly states guarding the eastern approaches to France, each providing a contingent of men trained according to the French principles of war. By 1809 the Confederation brought together 36 separate kingdoms, duchies and principalities under the eagle of France.

After the great successes of 1805, the Grande Armée had had little time to rest. Napoleon's continued insistence to impose harsh terms on those he defeated, either militarily or diplomatically, caused Prussia to rise against him in 1806. Although not involved in the fighting of 1805, Prussia had supported the Allies, causing Napoleon to humiliate Prussia diplomatically. Pushed too far, Prussia prepared for war, forming a new alliance with Russia in the process. Napoleon learned of this change quite late, but while the Prussians dithered, Napoleon swept into action.

On learning that the Prussian army was acting independently of their Russian allies, he grasped the opportunity to drive a wedge between the two and launched the Grande Armée forward. Six days later the Prussians had been crushed at the twin battle of Jena-Auerstädt, and in the general pursuit that followed, most of their army were captured, bringing the campaign to a close a month later. Once again, as in 1805, the rapidly moving French army had destroyed its opponents.

The army was now tired. In 14 months it had marched from the English Channel and fought the campaigns of Ulm, Austerlitz and Jena. New conscripts were arriving for service, but to make up for losses, numbers of Dutch and Spanish troops were also called forward for service on the long lines of communication. However, Napoleon had not finished: now he prepared to carry the war to the Russians. Denied any rest, the army advanced into Poland where it encountered this new enemy. Following a series of disjointed actions, the Russians withdrew. With the weather fast deteriorating, Napoleon finally allowed his men to move into winter quarters and rest. However, their opponents had other ideas. In mid-January 1807 the Russians advanced again and re-opened hostilities, leading to the bloody and terrible Battle of Eylau in February. In

Emperor Napoleon (1769-1821). At the beginning of 1809 Napoleon was at the height of his military power. He had defeated a Russo-Austrian army in 1805, the Prussians in 1806 and Russia in 1807. Now he was about to conduct campaigns on two fronts, as the war in Spain escalated and Austria again prepared to fight.

freezing temperatures amid the ice and snow, the two armies (the Russians with Prussian support) threw themselves at one another until neither side could do more. The casualties were horrendous. At the end of the second day the Russians chose to retire, but the French had been checked and were in no position to pursue. Napoleon returned his men to winter quarters.

Emerging in May to resume hostilities, Napoleon again encountered the Russians on a number of occasions but failed to bring them to conclusive battle until the evening of 13 June 1807. Then, at Friedland, the two adversaries became locked in desperate combat again until Napoleon emerged once more as the victor.

After two years of hard marching and fierce fighting, Napoleon and the Grande Armée were masters of all Europe. They had defeated the great powers of Austria, Prussia and Russia, one after the other, but Napoleon's army was no longer the finely honed weapon that had marched from the

AUSTRIAN INFANTRY ENTERING BAVARIA

The Austrian army crossed the border into Bavaria on 10 April. Unopposed, the army marched westwards in atrocious weather on roads turned into rivers of mud. Supplies became bogged down and disease took hold. III Korps initially suffered from poor march discipline too as civilian contractors forced their way into the main column and disrupted progress. This was only rectified following FML Rosenberg's personal intervention.

Channel ports in 1805. Those two years of fighting had claimed many casualties, brave men who would no longer return to their places in Napoleon's columns and lines. Instead, the veterans were joined by ever greater numbers of young conscripts; and with them came increasing numbers of foreign allies. Among these allies, the Confederation of the Rhine troops were now invaluable, and they took pride of place alongside Italians, Poles, Portuguese and Corsicans. Even from material as diverse as this, Napoleon was able to forge a new, strong and effective army. It lacked the elan of the armies of 1805 and 1806, but under Napoleon's hand it was still a powerful weapon, to be feared by all who encountered it.

OPENING PLANS

THE LULL BEFORE THE STORM

As the vast Austrian army assembled, fresh doubts began to enter Charles' mind, this time about the wisdom of an advance from Bohemia. Deficiencies in supplies and equipment for the army were becoming obvious as the component parts converged, and once again he questioned the readiness of his forces. Furthermore, the spectre of a largely unopposed French advance on Vienna, south of the Danube, haunted his deliberations. The plan for an advance north of the river began to present a number of irreconcilable risks, while a move south of the Danube appeared to be safer and offer greater protection to the capital. Despite strong opposition, Charles was determined to redefine his axis of advance, and on 13 March the great redeployment of the army began.

The escalating crisis in Spain had required Napoleon's presence there early in November 1808. However, it was not long before rumours reached him of increased Austrian military activity. By January he was convinced that Austria was preparing to embark on a new campaign in the spring. Warning orders were sent to the French troops still in Germany – mainly of Davout's III Corps – to begin to concentrate. Aware of the shortage of French soldiers in the central European theatre, in mid-January Napoleon wrote to the Rheinbund monarchs advising them to prepare for mobilisation. On 24 January 1809 Napoleon arrived back in Paris, having left the army in Spain under the command of Soult. He then increased his limited manpower by ordering the enrolment of great numbers of conscripts before their time. He had already plundered this source, but he was forced to take more. Thus he was able to create two new corps (II and IV) from the stockpile of manpower he had assembled. IV Corps, commanded by Massena, comprised French, Baden and Hessen-Darmstadt troops, while the Bavarians, Württembergers and Saxons were each formed into corps of their own (VII, VIII and IX). In addition, Napoleon was able to scrape together some reserve formations. The Imperial Guard, serving in Spain, were alerted to prepare for transfer to Germany. Other forces were gathered in the secondary theatres – Italy, Dalmatia and Poland. Napoleon elected to remain in Paris fearing that news of his arrival in Germany could hasten the onset of an Austrian offensive. Napoleon's chief of staff, Berthier, based in Strasbourg, was acting army commander.

During late February and early March the French and Allied troops began to move on the Upper Danube region. Napoleon felt that from this position, once he had arrested the initial Austrian attack, he would be able to turn defence to attack and move along the Danube valley to Vienna. To shield this concentration south of the Danube, the Bavarian

Marshal Berthier, Prince de Neuchâtel (1753-1815). Berthier was one of the great administrators of Napoleon's army, but lacked skill as a military commander. As chief-of-staff to the army, he was given temporary command of the army on the Danube in 1809. He found it difficult to interpret Napoleon's orders and was greatly relieved when the emperor arrived to take command. (ASKB)

VII Corps were pushed forward to the line of the Iser river. Having considered all the information he had before him and adding certain assumptions of his own, he felt it unlikely that Charles would be able to begin his offensive prior to 15 April. Should that be the case, he informed Berthier, the army would centre on Regensburg (known as Ratisbon to the French) at that date. However, should the Austrians move earlier, then Donauwörth and the river Lech, further to the west, were to be the focal point. All the information Napoleon had up to the end of March suggested that the main Austrian thrust would come from Bohemia, north of the Danube. At the end of the month Napoleon's newly created force, which had grown rapidly to a strength of approximately 170,000 men, was named La Grande Armée de L'Allemagne.

With confirmation of the realignment of the Austrian offensive, four of the korps formed in Bohemia (III, IV, V and I Reserve) received orders on 13 March to commence the long, tiring march southwards. It was cold, wet and miserable. V Korps, centred on Prague, had furthest to march: some 300km to reach their new assembly area. Charles could now count on about 127,000 men to form his main army, while the two korps which remained north of the Danube (I and II) mustered just under 50,000. Charles later wrote that despite their trials, the individual regiments of the army were "filled with the best spirit. There was greater order, discipline and mobility than before". However, and crucially, the move had given Napoleon three to four extra weeks in which to prepare his army for the coming war. However, despite reports in late March of a possible southern shift of the main Austrian strike force, Napoleon was still greatly surprised when he heard his opponents had crossed the Inn river, the border between Austria and Bavaria, on 10 April, five days ahead of the time he had predicted.

Napoleon's instructions regarding the crucial date of 15 April were despatched to Berthier on 30 March. Davout's III Corps were to concentrate towards Regensburg, then, once the city was occupied, Berthier was to move his headquarters forward to Ingolstadt, suggesting that Napoleon still felt the Austrians would not attack before 15 April. On 10 April Napoleon telegraphed further instructions to Berthier, expressing his view that the Austrians were about to attack. Indeed, that was the actual day they crossed the Inn. The telegram confirmed to Berthier that if the Austrians were about to attack, before 15 April, then the army was to draw back from the forward areas and deploy in the area around Donauwörth and Augsberg.

Unfortunately these clear instructions failed to reach Berthier until early morning on 16 April, six days later. By then the French and Allied forces had embarked on a series of marches and counter-marches which had left the army disgruntled and in confusion: Berthier was totally out of his depth. This confusion had arisen because a written order expanding on the telegram of 10 April, despatched by courier at the same time, arrived 55 hours earlier than the telegram itself. The despatch stated that a copy of the telegram was enclosed, but it was not. Without the telegram, Berthier misinterpreted Napoleon's instructions. In fact, most of the contents of the letter more or less conformed to the orders Berthier had issued once he had heard that the Austrians had crossed the Inn. However, the letter then returned to the matter of the possibility of the Austrians not attacking before 15 April, in which case Davout was to remain in Regensburg with his corps, all within one day's march of the city, and then followed the words "...and that under all circumstances". Without the telegram which specifically ordered the whole army to concentrate on Donauwörth and the Lech, Berthier was confused: lacking this crucial information, he decided to give great importance to remaining in Regensburg "under all circumstances". Davout at this point was already pulling back in the direction of Ingolstadt when the order, based on this misinterpretation, arrived from Berthier instructing him to return to Regensburg. This he reluctantly did.

The two wings of the army were now separated by about 120km of Bavarian countryside, linked only by the three Bavarian divisions of VII Corps behind the Iser river. On the evening of 14 April a despairing Berthier wrote to Napoleon: "In this position of affairs, I greatly desire the arrival of your Majesty." His salvation was at hand: Napoleon had left Paris in the early hours of 13 April.

Generalleutnant Wrede, commander of Bavarian 2nd Division of VII Corps. Wrede's men were subject to a series of confusing and contradictory orders in the opening stages of the campaign. Moving back and forwards between Straubing on the Danube and Abensberg, they made no significant contact with the Austrians.

etween 3.00 and 4.00am on the morning of 10 April the Austrian army advanced into Bavaria. At Schärding, on the right, first to cross the Inn were GM Vécsey's brigade detached from II Korps, followed by IV Korps (FML Rosenberg) and I Reserve Korps (GdK Liechtenstein). At Mulheim III Korps (FML Hohenzollern) crossed via a pontoon bridge, and on the left at Braunau VI Korps (FML Hiller) were followed by V Korps (FML Archduke Louis). II Reserve Korps were held back for the time being. On the extreme left a division detached from the main body of VI Korps, commanded by FML Jellacic, were positioned at Salzburg, ready to advance towards the Bavarian capital, Munich. Meanwhile, the two korps north of the Danube, I Korps (GdK Bellegarde) and II Korps (FZM Kolowrat), debouched from Bohemia and moved westwards. The advance guards of each korps pushed forward enthusiastically, seeking information about the movements of their enemy. The only opposition they encountered was provided by the weather, which was atrocious. It was very cold, and snow mixed with the rain to make life very uncomfortable for everyone.

The nightmare march continued in much the same vein for the following two days; the rain continued, columns lost their way and march discipline was initially poor. The artillery and transport became bogged down continually on the wretched roads and could not keep up. The army was suffering; the cold, the wet, the mud and the lack of supplies soon led to outbreaks of typhoid.

On 13 April Charles found it necessary to call a day of rest. The army needed a chance to recover and it was essential that the transport and supply wagons closed up. The weather showed some temporary improvement, allowing the men the opportunity to clean their weapons and equipment and to repair their shoes, which were suffering greatly. Having been resupplied, the army marched off again the following day, and the rain returned. Patrols of opposing Austrian and Bavarian cavalry began to make contact. A few shots were exchanged and prisoners taken. Progress was again slow, but by the evening of 15 April the army was within a short march of the Iser, while some advance units were already on its banks.

THE SKIES DARKEN:
THE FIRST BATTLE OF LANDSHUT

Sunday 16 April dawned bright and sunny. It was a welcome change for the soldiers of both sides, who had endured a miserable week. This was the day the war would escalate; Charles was to force the passage of the Iser.

Generalleutnant Deroy, commander of Bavarian 3rd Division of VII Corps. Deroy's Division was the first to encounter the advancing Austrians at the opening of the campaign. He opposed the crossing of the Iser river at Landshut, until his position was in danger of being outflanked, whereupon he withdrew.

On the right FML Rosenberg was to lead IV Korps across the river at Dingolfing. On the left FML Hiller was to move with VI Korps to the river at Moosberg. The main column, with V Korps at its head, was to form on the Landshut road, about 10km from the town. Behind them III Korps was tasked with a supporting role. I and II Reserve Korps were to follow on behind. A patrol from V Korps Advance Guard had entered Landshut on the previous day and found the two main bridges partly broken. Bavarian troops were guarding the bridges, and the Austrians tried unsuccessfully to negotiate a peaceful handover. Around dawn the next day the bulk of GM Radetzky's advance guard marched into town.

The road into Landshut from the south passed Traunsitz castle on the heights, some 70-80m above the river, then descended to the town below. The first bridge, the Lend, crossed the single channel of the Iser west of the main town and allowed access to the northern suburb of St. Nikolai without the need to traverse the town centre. Continuing along the road from the Lend bridge, the tall buildings on either side of the road led to the Spital bridge. At this point the river had divided into two channels, separated by a built-up island known as Zwischenbrücken. From here another bridge connected the island with the suburbs of Seelingthal and St. Nikolai. Beyond the town the wide sodden plain of the Iser valley extended for about 3km north, before it gently rose again beyond the villages of Altdorf and Ergolding.

The troops defending the Landshut river crossing were of Generalleutnant Deroy's Bavarian 3rd Division of VII Corps. They had arrived at Landshut in the early hours of 15 April with orders to defend the crossing. If faced by overwhelming numbers, they were not to offer a determined resistance but to withdraw. Against Deroy's force of just under 10,000 men, Archduke Charles was leading about 25,000 men of V Korps, supported by 26,000 of III Korps.

The Bavarian front-line defence was provided by the division's 1st Brigade who defended the river crossings and suburbs of Landshut. The rest of the division were drawn up to the rear at Altdorf, protecting the line of retreat. As soon as Radetzky arrived in Landshut, he again attempted to persuade the Bavarians to withdraw. They refused, and at about 10.00am, when the head of V Korps arrived, with nerves already strained, the pickets opened fire and the battle began. Bullets, shot and shell flew furiously across the Iser. The superior weight of Austrian firepower began to take its toll, forcing the Bavarians back from the river's edge. News then filtered through to Deroy that another Austrian force (Hiller's VI Korps) had crossed the Iser at Moosberg and thus threatened his right flank. Wisely Deroy ordered a withdrawal. The Bavarians fell back, largely unmolested, as the Austrians filed over the rapidly repaired bridges. Austrian cavalry caught up with the Bavarian rearguard near Altdorf and a fierce mêlée developed. However, as Austrian infantry approached, the Bavarian cavalry broke off the combat and followed their retreating division up the road towards Siegenburg.

Back in Landshut, Charles could feel pleased with the efforts of the day. With only minimal casualties his men had forced the Iser river crossing. He was delighted with the performance of his light troops, cavalry and artillery, and felt that the new-found enthusiasm of the army was much in evidence. An eyewitness described the town as "packed full of troops, who sang Bohemian and Slavic war songs... the Austrians streamed through the town in a steady flow, quite splendid cavalry, a continual 'Hurrah' for Archduke Charles, who looked full of courage and seriousness". But the situation was about to change dramatically. At 5.00am the following morning Napoleon rode into Donauwörth and took direct control of the army.

STORM CLOUDS GATHER: NAPOLEON TAKES COMMAND

On his arrival in Donauwörth, Napoleon was angered to find that Berthier was in Augsburg. Although he had received reports during his journey to the front, Napoleon had by no means a complete picture of his own army's position and only a confused impression of Austrian intentions. However, news came in from Massena of the position on the Lech, and direct contact was made with Vandamme, while Lefebvre with the Bavarians was presumed to be pulling back across the Abens river towards the Ilm. By mid-morning Napoleon had news of Davout and learned that part of III Corps were holding Regensburg. Quickly realising that his army was in a weak position, thinly spread over a wide area, he selected the city of Ingolstadt as the place of concentration for the army. At about 10.00am Napoleon learned that an Austrian korps of unknown size had forced the Iser at Landshut. About an hour later he issued the orders detailing the concentration of the army, which was to take place the following day, 18 April. The key elements of these orders were that Davout, on the left, was to withdraw from Regensburg and unite with Lefebvre's Bavarians close to the junction of the Danube and Abens rivers, while Massena and Oudinot, on the right, were to establish themselves at Pfaffenhofen on the Ilm. Then, by the morning of 19 April, with Davout having moved to Geisenfeld on the Ilm, south-east of Ingolstadt, Napoleon would be ready to go over to the offensive with his army in three great masses – Davout (III Corps) at Geisenfeld, Vandamme (VIII Corps) and the divisions of Demont, Rouyer and Nansouty around Ingolstadt, and Massena and Oudinot (IV and II corps) at Pfaffenhofen. Lefebvre (VII Corps) would then cover the left of the army on a front of about 25km. First, the Bavarians would be required to hold the Austrians advancing from Landshut to protect Davout's withdrawal. However, there were flaws in these orders. Napoleon believed erroneously that only one Austrian korps was advancing from Landshut, Davout was not able to concentrate his corps at Regensburg until 19 April, and Massena and Oudinot's corps were also widely spread; it would only be possible for advance elements of these corps to arrive at Pfaffenhofen by the prescribed time.

CHARLES PUSHES ON TOWARDS THE DANUBE

For Charles, the result of the action at Landshut did little to clarify his opponents' intentions. On the evening of 16 April he wrote: "My operation will probably be directed toward the Danube, where the enemy

Marshal Davout, Duc d'Auerstädt (1770-1823), commander of III Corps. The orders issued by Napoleon on 17 April instructed Davout to march from Regensburg and join Lefebvre the next day. Davout was not able to commence his march until 19 April, so found himself exposed to an Austrian attack. (P. Haythornthwaite)

appears to be massing his main forces. I cannot determine their actual direction just at the moment."

Charles did not immediately follow up his advantage over the Bavarians, and used 17 April to form up the army across the Iser and prepare it for the next advance. While this repositioning of the army was carried out, extensive reconnaissance patrols probed forward. Carefully examining and analysing the information these patrols had gleaned, a clearer picture of the position of the French and Allied army began to form. It appeared to Austrian headquarters that Davout was facing the two korps of Bellegarde to the north of Regensburg, and that the Bavarians were continuing to retreat beyond the Abens, towards the Danube. It was

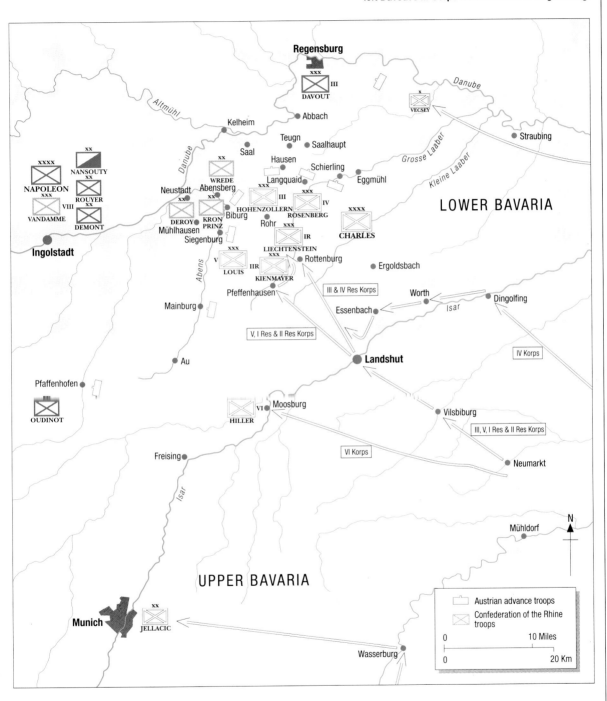

ISOLATION OF DAVOUT

The Austrian line of advance into Bavaria and the positions of both armies during the night of 18-19 April 1809. The Austrian push towards the Danube left Davout's III Corps isolated south of Regensburg.

also known that there were forces on the Lech and around Donauwörth which were possibly pulling further upstream. Therefore, besides those on the Lech around Augsburg, the main enemy forces appeared to be spread in a long cordon along the northern bank of the Danube, with an attempt at concentration between Ingolstadt and Regensburg.

The opportunity for a great victory appeared to be presenting itself to Charles. If he pushed the army on now and forced a crossing of the Danube near Kelheim, he thought he could break the cordon and force Davout to withdraw on the Rhine. Then, by continuing to advance northwards, he could force the French to abandon their position on the Lech and evacuate large areas of southern Germany. Determined to grasp this opportunity, Charles issued his orders for 18 April. As there were only two roads from Landshut that would allow the army to move north-west towards the Abens, the main advance was to be in two large columns. One road was via Rottenburg and Rohr, the other ran through Pfeffenhausen. This axis of advance had the benefit of drawing the main army closer to the two korps operating north of the Danube. On the right III Korps were to march from Landshut up the Rottenburg road followed by IV Korps. On the left V Korps were to lead, followed by I and II Reserve Korps. On the extreme right Vécsey's detached brigade from II Korps was to demonstrate towards Regensburg and attempt to establish the enemy strength there, while on the far left VI Korps were to carry out a slow march towards Pfaffenhofen.

Meanwhile, north of the Danube, the hesitating advance of I and II Korps continued, leading to an advance guard probing towards Regensburg on 17 April. At Rheinhausen, just to the north, French and Austrian skirmishers clashed and artillery exchanged fire. Davout had received orders to march from Regensburg on 18 April, but as he could not concentrate his corps in time, he planned to delay his march until the following day.

CHARLES LEARNS OF DAVOUT'S ISOLATION

On the morning of 18 April the Austrian korps returned to the advance as ordered, but shortly after the march commenced, Charles received intelligence which made it necessary to cancel all existing orders. The report stated that Davout had a force of about 30,000 men, and a part of it had marched out of Regensburg and was encamped in woodland south of the city. This dramatic development suggested that the idea that the French were concentrating north of the Danube was false. Whether Davout intended linking up with the Bavarians or the French were switching to the offensive could not be determined. However, what was apparent to Charles was that Davout presented a target that could be attacked with an overwhelming force. By 10.00am on the morning of 18 April Charles had issued new orders for a concentration of three korps on Rohr. From there, an attack could be made on Davout. III Korps and IV Korps, along with I Reserve Korps, strengthened by the attachment of Lindenau's Division from V Korps and a cavalry brigade from II Reserve Korps, were designated for the task. The rest of V Korps and the remaining elements of II Reserve Korps, now all commanded by Archduke Louis (Erzherzog Ludwig), were to protect the left flank of the force marching on Rohr, while Hiller was to secure Louis' left. North of the Danube desultory fighting had continued throughout the day, as the last elements of Davout's corps passed across the river and through Regensburg.

BATTLE OF TEUGN-HAUSEN
19 APRIL 1809

LOCATING THE ENEMY

That evening, at his headquarters in Rohr, Charles issued orders for the following day, which were intended to locate and defeat Davout's III Corps (one of the finest in the French army). In the early hours of 19 April Charles received further intelligence which suggested that Lefebvre's Bavarians were ready to offer support to Davout. Determined to pin Davout with the Danube at his back and make it impossible for him to evade battle, Charles opened out the korps encamped at Rohr into a converging cordon. Liechtenstein, with his I Reserve Korps (8,800 men and 4,100 cavalry), strengthened by the addition of Vécsey's brigade (5,200 men and 900 cavalry), was to march

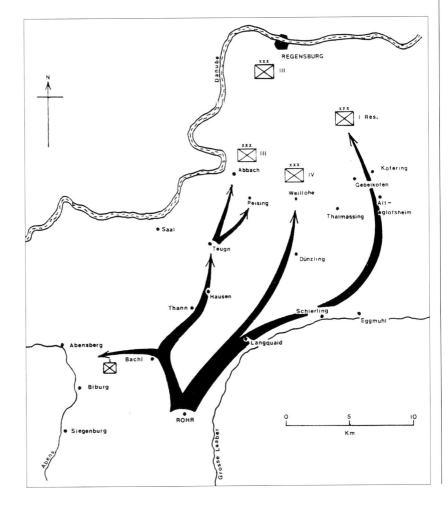

Archduke Charles' plan for the location and defeat of Davout's III Corps, 19 April 1809. Aware that Davout was now to the south of Regensburg, Charles changed his plans, ordering I Reserve Korps from Rohr towards Regensburg, IV Korps towards Weillohe and III Korps to Abbach and Peising, hoping to catch Davout in this converging cordon.

10ème LÉGÈRE AT TEUGN-HAUSEN

The 10ème Légère had initially passed through the village of Teugn but were recalled. Advancing on the right of the line the 10ème moved into the woods to their front, where they engaged a battalion of Austrian grenzer. Supported by a battalion of 3ème Ligne they forced the grenzer to give ground, then, advancing further through the woods, the 10ème threatened the flank of an Austrian battery, forcing it to withdraw.

from Rohr towards Regensburg. Rosenberg, with IV Korps and the grenadiers, which were now detached from I Reserve Korps (total strength 27,000 men and 2,200 cavalry), were to march for Weillohe. Hohenzollern's III Korps (20,100 men and 1,050 cavalry) would move to Teugn, where it was to split into two columns and move on Peising and Abbach. A brigade commanded by GM Thierry was to be detached to a position between Abensberg and Biburg to protect the rear of the korps. Louis, with V Korps and II Reserve Korps (15,800 men and 2,900 cavalry) on the Pfeffenhausen–Siegenburg road, was to push forward to Siegenburg. They were to be joined by Hiller and VI Korps (23,600 men and 2,200 cavalry). Once in position, Hiller was to assume command of this wing of the army and be prepared to counter any aggressive move by Lefebvre's Bavarians.

Davout had also issued his orders on the evening of 18 April. The corps train was to follow the road which ran along the south bank of the Danube towards Abensberg. Marching to the east of it were two columns. The first was formed by the men of Morand and St. Hilaire's Divisions with cavalry support. To their east the second column was formed by the divisions of Gudin and Friant, also supported by cavalry. These columns marched at 5.00am. The 65ème Légère were left behind to garrison Regensburg. By 8.30am Morand's Division, leading the right-hand column, had reached Teugn, while to the east Gudin's men had arrived at Saalhaupt accompanied by Davout. On arrival, Davout was alerted that Austrian units had been seen advancing between Bachl and Langquaid, threatening the Abensberg road. To protect his valuable train, Davout despatched Morand and Gudin's Divisions to move westwards through Teugn.

25

Charles too, accompanying IV Korps, had been alerted to the proximity of the enemy, and he halted in battle order between the tiny villages of Grub and Leierndorf (Leyendorf), awaiting the appearance of III Korps on his left. As the lead elements of III Korps arrived before the village of Hausen, Rosenberg was able to continue his advance with IV Korps towards Dünzling (Dinzling). However, he reduced the strength of his command by making a number of detachments. Charles remained at Grub with the grenadiers because of the fighting which had started nearby at Hausen.

Hohenzollern's III Korps had begun their march from Rohr between 7.00 and 8.00am on 19 April. Leaving a small detachment under GM Pfanzelter in the village of Bachl, advance patrols of the korps approached Hausen and found it to be in French hands. To clear the village, FML Lusignan led GM Kayser's brigade forward. Meanwhile, a battalion of 9. Peterwardein Grenzer skirted to the west of

FML Hohenzollern-Hechingen, commander of III Korps. On the morning of 19 April he was heading for Teugn as part of Charles' attempt to envelop Davout. However, Hohenzollern ran into part of Davout's corps at Hausen, and the initial clash developed into the battle of Teugn-Hausen.

ORDER OF BATTLE
Teugn-Hausen, 19 April 1809

AUSTRIAN ARMY

III KORPS
Commander: Feldmarschalleutnant (FML) Hohenzollern-Hechingen
Total strength approx. 16,420 infantry, 780 cavalry, 52 guns

Advance Guard: FML Vukassovich
II Bat. 9. Peterwardein Grenzer
I Bat. Erzherzog Karl Legion (Waltrich Jäger)
3. Erzherzog Ferdinand Husaren (6 sqdn)
Cavalry battery (4 x 6pdr. and 2 x 7pdr. howitzers)

Division: FML Lusignan
Brigade: Generalmajor (GM) Kayser
IR7 Schröder (2 and 2/3 Bat. [16 coys])
IR56 Colloredo (2 and 5/6 Bat. [17 coys])
Brigade battery (8 x 6pdr.)

Division: FML St. Julien
Brigade: GM Alois Liechtenstein
IR12 Manfredini (2 and 2/3 Bat. [16 coys])
IR23 Würzburg (2 Bat. [12 coys])
Brigade battery (8 x 6pdr.)

Brigade: GM Bieber
IR20 Kaunitz (2 and 2/3 Bat. [16 coys])
IR38 Württemburg (2 Bat. [12 coys])
Brigade battery (8 x 6pdr.)

Reserve Artillery: Oberst Smola
Brigade battery (8 x 6pdr.)
Position battery (4 x 6pdr. and 2 x 7pdr. howitzers)
1/2 Position battery (2 x 6pdr.)
Position battery (4 x 12pdr. and 2 x 7pdr. howitzers)

Hausen and moved through the intervening woods towards Roith. However, with the approach of Kayser's brigade the French, mainly foraging parties, swiftly moved out and escaped northwards into the trees. Unopposed, the brigade occupied the village while the rest of the korps formed on the high ground to the rear between Thann and Hausen.

Hausen was a small village resting on a ridge. Beyond the village the ground sloped gently down to a small stream before rising steeply to the next ridge, the Hausener Berg. Thick woodland closed in on either side of the road as it climbed the slope, but the summit itself was clear and open. From the Hausener Berg the ground sloped away again before climbing once more to the Buchberg, the next hilltop in this green, rolling countryside, which overlooked and sheltered the village of Teugn.

TEUGN-HAUSEN

Hohenzollern and Davout clash between the villages of Teugn and Hausen as Charles' converging cordon marches northwards.

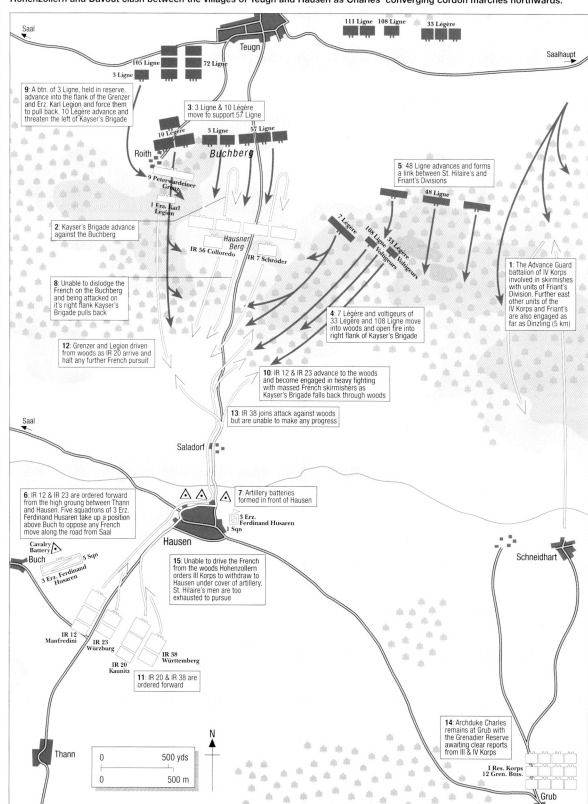

Saal

Saalhaupt

111 Ligne   108 Ligne   33 Légère

Teugn

105 Ligne   72 Ligne

3 Ligne

9: A btn. of 3 Ligne, held in reserve, advance into the flank of the Grenzer and Erz. Karl Legion and force them to pull back. 10 Légère advance and threaten the left of Kayser's Brigade

3: 3 Ligne & 10 Légère move to support 57 Ligne

10 Légère   3 Ligne   57 Ligne

Roith

Buchberg

5: 48 Ligne advances and forms a link between St. Hilaire's and Friant's Divisions

48 Ligne

9 Peterwardeiner Grenz

1 Erz. Karl Legion

2: Kayser's Brigade advance against the Buchberg

7 Légère   108 Ligne Voltigeurs   33 Légère Voltigeurs

Hausner Berg

IR 56 Colloredo   IR 7 Schröder

1: The Advance Guard battalion of IV Korps involved in skirmishes with units of Friant's Division. Further east other units of the IV Korps and Friant's are also engaged as far as Dinzling (5 km)

8: Unable to dislodge the French on the Buchberg and being attacked on it's right flank Kayser's Brigade pulls back

4: 7 Légère and voltigeurs of 33 Légère and 108 Ligne move into woods and open fire into right flank of Kayser's Brigade

12: Grenzer and Legion driven from woods as IR 20 arrive and halt any further French pursuit

10: IR 12 & IR 23 advance to the woods and become engaged in heavy fighting with massed French skirmishers as Kayser's Brigade falls back through woods

13: IR 38 joins attack against woods but are unable to make any progress

Saal

Saladorf

6: IR 12 & IR 23 are ordered forward from the high groung between Thann and Hausen. Five squadrons of 3 Erz. Ferdinand Husaren take up a position above Buch to oppose any French move along the road from Saal

7: Artillery batteries formed in front of Hausen

3 Erz. Ferdinand Husaren
1 Sqn

Hausen

Schneidhart

Cavalry Battery   5 Sqn

Buch

3 Erz. Ferdinand Husaren

15: Unable to drive the French from the woods Hohenzollern orders III Korps to withdraw to Hausen under cover of artillery. St. Hilaire's men are too exhausted to pursue

IR 12 Manfredini

IR 23 Würzburg

IR 20 Kaunitz

IR 38 Württemberg

11: IR 20 & IR 38 are ordered forward

14: Archduke Charles remains at Grub with the Grenadier Reserve awaiting clear reports from III & IV Korps

Thann

N

0   500 yds

0   500 m

I Res. Korps
12 Gren. Btns.

Grub

THE BATTLE BEGINS

Sounds of firing could now be heard coming from the direction taken by IV Korps, but the nature of the ground made it impossible to determine exactly what was happening. So Hohenzollern decided to continue his march thereby assisting Rosenberg by advancing on his flank. A continuation of the advance would also keep him on target to operate against the Regensburg road, which was the main purpose of the morning's orders. After a short rest FML Lusignan was ordered to continue the march on Teugn, this time with the addition of a squadron of 3. Erzherzog Ferdinand-Husaren. Kayser's brigade was a strong one, being only three companies short of six full battalions. Sending skirmishers ahead, the long column marched up to the Hausener Berg unopposed, where the lead battalions deployed into battle order. Ahead of them came the sounds of gunfire: their skirmishers and Grenzer from Roith, having crossed the Buchberg and moved down into Teugn, had encountered French troops. Lusignan quickly pushed forward some supports for his skirmishers and formed the main body of his infantry and a brigade battery of 6pdrs on the Hausener Berg. The opponents that the skirmishers were engaging were the tail units of Gudin's Division. Morand's Division had already safely passed and were almost on the Regensburg–Abensberg road. The speed of the French marching had enabled half of Davout's corps to evade the tightening cordon. However, St. Hilaire's Division, which had marched behind Morand on the right, had been delayed, and now arrived at Teugn around 11.00am and marched into the fire of the Austrian skirmish line.

The action soon escalated. The 10ème Légère, the leading regiment of the division, had already moved through Teugn when Davout recognised the seriousness of the situation and recalled them. Then he

Battle of Teugn-Hausen, 19 April 1809 (known by the French as Thann, although no fighting took place near that village). In this illustration Austrian infantry skirmishes and Grenzers on the high ground above Teugn are firing down into Gudin and St. Hilaire's divisions of Davout's corps as they march .. .. the main Regensburg–Abensberg road. (ASKB)

rushed the three battalions of 3ème Ligne forward and up the northern ascent of the Buchberg, but because of their rapid deployment the breathless 3ème were easily repulsed by the skirmish line and their supports. Determined to secure his position, Davout ordered the last regiment of Lorencez's brigade, the 57ème Ligne, up the Buchberg, but made sure they were formed in tight columns. This time the French drove back the skirmish line and established themselves on the high ground, despite being assailed by heavy musketry, artillery fire and an attack by the squadron of Erzherzog Ferdinand-Husaren.

While the 57ème were carrying out their attack, St. Hilaire formed Destabenrath's brigade (72ème and 105ème Ligne) on the slopes north of Teugn. Confident that the situation had been stabilised, Davout felt he had time to ride after the divisions of Morand and Gudin and direct them in a flank attack against Hausen from the Abensberg road at Saal. But before he could issue the orders, a report reached him from St. Hilaire informing him that the Austrians were attacking again. Leaving Morand to secure the road, Davout turned about and rode hard for Teugn. In his absence Lusignan had led forward Kayser's brigade against the 57ème, supported by the battalion of Peterwardein Grenzer. The Grenzers, now themselves supported by 1. Erzherzog Karl Legion (Waltrich Jäger), had advanced again through the woods and were threatening the right flank of the 57ème. However, Lusignan was prevented from making a significant impression on the French line by the nature of the ground, which limited his ability to fully deploy. Concerned most immediately by the pressure being brought to bear by the Grenzer, Davout ordered two battalions of the 3ème to form on the right of the 57ème, and the 10ème Légère to move against the wood. The line was backed up by Destabenrath's brigade. A third battalion of the 3ème then advanced on Roith and swung into the woodland on the village's eastern flank, cutting off and capturing a number of the Grenzer. Those remaining fell back to a line in the trees south of Roith, still supported by the Erzherzog Karl Legion. The danger to the French right flank had been removed.

Austrian skirmishers' view from the Buchberg looking towards Teugn. The attack by 57ème Ligne in columns came up the road from the village which runs by the line of trees in the centre of the photo. This attack was successful: the 57ème drove the Austrian light troops off the Buchberg.

The battlefield of Teugn-Hausen. Taken from the Austrian position on the Hausner Berg looking north towards the Buchberg. The woods in the distance on the left of the Buchberg are those from which the Grenzers fired on the 57ème. Kayser's Brigade retreated back up the slope in the foreground, followed by the French.

BELOW The battlefield of Teugn-Hausen. Taken from the western end of the Buchberg, where it joins the woods. This was the position occupied by 3ème Ligne. The high ground to the right of centre, where it is clear of trees, is the Hausener Berg, from where Austrian III Korps began its attack. The tree line on the left marks the woods from which French light infantry threatened the right of the Austrian line.

Now Lusignan was in trouble. Hohenzollern was at this time still behind Hausen with the rest of the infantry about nine battalions of FML St. Julien's Division. He had been reluctant to throw everything at the French line because the rolling wooded terrain concealed the enemy's true strength. Lusignan appealed for support, which Hohenzollern sent forward in the form of GM Alois Liechtenstein's brigade (IR12 Manfredini and two battalions of IR23 Würzburg). The battalions advancing laboriously in battalion columns were ordered to move into the woods to the right of the road. However, their move was too little too late. Kayser's brigade had been forced to give ground due to mounting pressure to their front and flanks, as first the Grenzers had been pushed back on the left and then increasing numbers of French skirmishers

appeared on the right. These were the first units from Friant's Division that had arrived at Saalhaupt. At this village they ran into part of IV Korps' advance guard which was attempting to reach Abbach, and were forced to feed large numbers of men into the woods south of the village to prevent a threat developing against their flank as they turned towards Teugn. Friant's Division was somewhat weakened by these detachments by the time it took up a position in reserve to the east of this village.

The first to move against the right flank of III Korps were the voltigeurs of 33ème Ligne. Shortly after, they were joined by GB Petit, who had been leading a battalion of 7ème Légère in advance of Gudin's Division. Petit had been thrown back to Saalhaupt by IV Korps' advance guard, and was now marching to rejoin his Division. However, Davout stopped him on the road and sent him, with his battalion and the voltigeurs of 108ème Ligne, to join the 33ème. Now assailed from front and flank in strength, Kayser's brigade, amid mounting casualties, including Lusignan himself, fell back through the woods on the Hausener Berg. Pursued by the French, a bloody fight developed among the trees, but the French tactics were far superior in this type of terrain. Kayser's men were pushed out of the southern edge of the wood, on the slopes above Hausen, just as IR12 Manfredini were advancing towards it. The French, now lining the edge of the wood, supported by artillery were able to bring a heavy fire to bear against IR12 as it advanced towards the wood.

The fighting in and around the woods was very confused, and detailed reports are not available, but it is possible that the regiment penetrated into the woods. To their support, Alois Liechtenstein, grasping the standard of IR23 Würzburg, led that regiment forward with elements from the re-forming IR7 and IR56. They moved against the salient of trees close to the eastern side of the road, from where a heavy fire was being directed against the Austrian columns moving up the road. The attack pressed into the woods at the point of the bayonet but was repulsed, and the regiment fell back. Alois Liechtenstein was severely wounded.

While these attacks were in progress, Hohenzollern had been making efforts to secure his position by placing several batteries of artillery in front of Hausen. Cavalry and another battery had already been sent westwards to Buch to prevent any attempt by the French, now known to

THE ATTACK BY IR23 AT TEUGN-HAUSEN

Having repulsed the main Austrian assault towards the village of Teugn, the French pursued aggressively and occupied the woods on the Hausener Berg, the high ground overlooking Hausen. IR12 were ordered to attack the French, who were now lining the southern edge of the wood, in an attempt to drive them back. IR23 Würzburg advanced in support, led forward by Gen.Maj. Alois Liechtenstein brandishing their standard. Although they broke into the woods, they were eventually forced out and fell back. Liechtenstein was severely wounded for his efforts.

be at Saal, advancing against Hausen from that direction. Hohenzollern himself then led IR20 Kaunitz into the fray on the left, just as a threat there developed when the Peterwardein Grenzer and Erzherzog Karl Legion were ejected from the woods west of the road. Two battalions of IR38 Württemburg, the last of the uncommitted reserves, were then sent forward on the right, but could do nothing to tip the balance back in Austrian favour as the determined French clung on to their position in the woods. It was now 3.00pm and Hohenzollern accepted that he could not recapture the woods. He ordered his men back to Hausen, where they re-formed under cover of his well-positioned batteries. The French, exhausted by the long battle, showed no inclination to interfere.

Throughout the day Charles had remained in position with the grenadiers at Grub, just 4km away. He had been reluctant to enter the conflict at Hausen because he believed that battle was flaring all along the line and he was awaiting a clear indication of the overall situation before committing these reserves. None arrived. Eventually, too late to have any impact on the action, Charles moved with the grenadiers to Hausen. Firing was already dying out by this time and a fierce thunderstorm which had been threatening all day finally broke, bringing down the curtain on a day that had promised a great victory for Charles but had only delivered defeat.

The great plan to intercept Davout had failed badly. Now there was nothing to stop the commander of III Corps from linking up with the Bavarians and strengthening the French-Allied position. Demoralised by the defeat, Charles felt he needed to shift the army back to a more secure position. Hohenzollern's III Korps, after resting for the night at Hausen, marched eastwards to Leierndorf. Rosenberg's IV Korps, which had been involved in inconclusive clashes all through the previous day (with Montbrun's Cavalry Division and advanced elements of Gudin's Division around Dünzling), were to remain in position and cover III Korps' move in the morning. Archduke Louis, with V Korps, was asked to march overnight through Rohr and Langquaid to link up with the main army, as Charles felt sure that the flames of battle would reignite the following day. Hiller, whose advanced detachments had encountered some French troops close to Pfaffenhofen the day before, was to move and occupy Louis' current position north-west of Pfeffenhausen. North of the Danube, attempts by Kolowrat's II Korps to force a passage across the river into Regensburg had been thwarted by the determined action of the three battalions of the 65ème Ligne regiment. Davout had originally instructed the regiment to hold the city until the evening and then follow the main body of the corps, but now word was sent to hold on at all costs. If that were not possible, at least the garrison were to destroy the massive stone bridge over the river. The confidence which had previously been prevalent at Austrian headquarters had now dissolved, and the initiative passed to Napoleon.

Generalmajor Alois Fürst Liechtenstein (1780-1833), commander of an infantry brigade in FML St. Julien's Division at Teugn-Hausen. Ordered forward in support of Kayser's brigade, Liechtenstein found Kayser already in retreat when he arrived. Undeterred, he grasped the standard of IR23 and bravely led them against the pursuing French infantry in the woods.

As Alois Liechtenstein led IR23 forward, he was severely wounded. In the same action, his brother, GM Moritz Fürst Liechtenstein, was also wounded. These two, the brothers of Johann Liechtenstein, commander of I Reserve Korps, were carried to safety on a cart and eventually recovered from their wounds. (ÖNB)

FRENCH AND AUSTRIAN REACTIONS TO THE BATTLE

Napoleon had spent much of 19 April at Ingolstadt, but during the afternoon he received a report from Davout detailing the battle that had just taken place. He then set up his headquarters at Vohburg. The previous day he had written to Massena, stressing the importance of his arrival at Pfaffenhofen with both II Corps and IV Corps as soon as possible, emphasising the need with the words: "Activity, activity, speed! I commend them to you." Recognising the urgency in Napoleon's communication, Massena forced his men on for two days. By the end of 19 April the great majority of the two corps were in the vicinity of Pfaffenhofen. During 19 April Napoleon wrote to Massena again, informing him that Davout was marching from Regensburg towards Neustädt, where he would link up with the Bavarians. By this move, Napoleon explained, he had refused his left, allowing him to advance with his right, namely Massena's command. Advancing towards Landshut, Massena would be able to place himself across Charles' line of communications. Massena was also instructed to order Oudinot to send one of his divisions to reinforce the build-up on the left.

Back at Vohburg, Napoleon, who had been joined by two more of his marshals, Lannes and Bessières, received a report from the Bavarians on the Abens that some Austrian units were advancing in their area. A fierce fight developed around Arnhofen, about 3km north-east of Abensberg, as GM Thierry's brigade, detached from III Korps, probed forward. Eventually Thierry's men were forced back to Offenstetten.

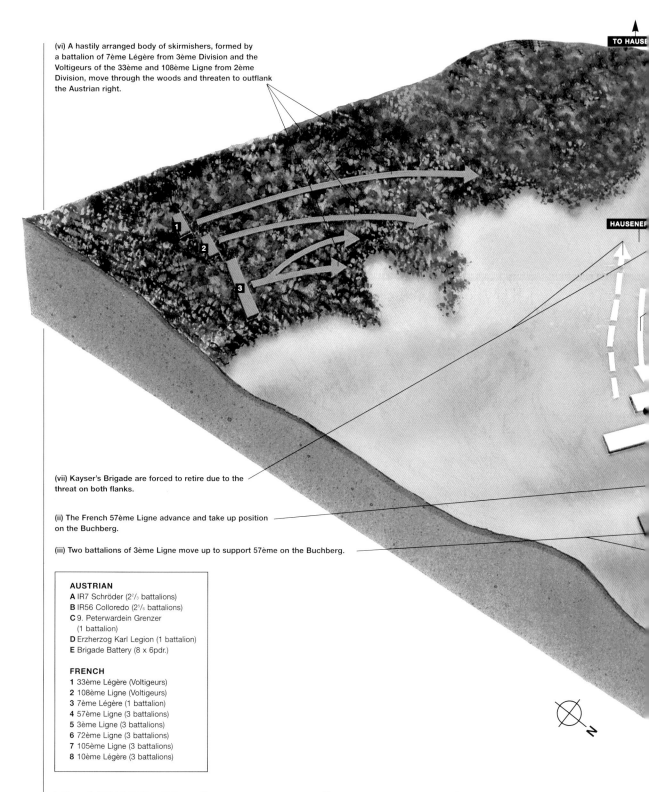

(vi) A hastily arranged body of skirmishers, formed by
a battalion of 7ème Légère from 3ème Division and the
Voltigeurs of the 33ème and 108ème Ligne from 2ème
Division, move through the woods and threaten to outflank
the Austrian right.

HAUSENER

(vii) Kayser's Brigade are forced to retire due to the
threat on both flanks.

(ii) The French 57ème Ligne advance and take up position
on the Buchberg.

(iii) Two battalions of 3ème Ligne move up to support 57ème on the Buchberg.

AUSTRIAN
A IR7 Schröder (2²/₃ battalions)
B IR56 Colloredo (2⁵/₆ battalions)
C 9. Peterwardein Grenzer
   (1 battalion)
D Erzherzog Karl Legion (1 battalion)
E Brigade Battery (8 x 6pdr.)

FRENCH
1 33ème Légère (Voltigeurs)
2 108ème Ligne (Voltigeurs)
3 7ème Légère (1 battalion)
4 57ème Ligne (3 battalions)
5 3ème Ligne (3 battalions)
6 72ème Ligne (3 battalions)
7 105ème Ligne (3 battalions)
8 10ème Légère (3 battalions)

BATTLE OF TEUGN-HAUSEN
19 APRIL 1809

The Austrian attempt to intercept Davout is repulsed

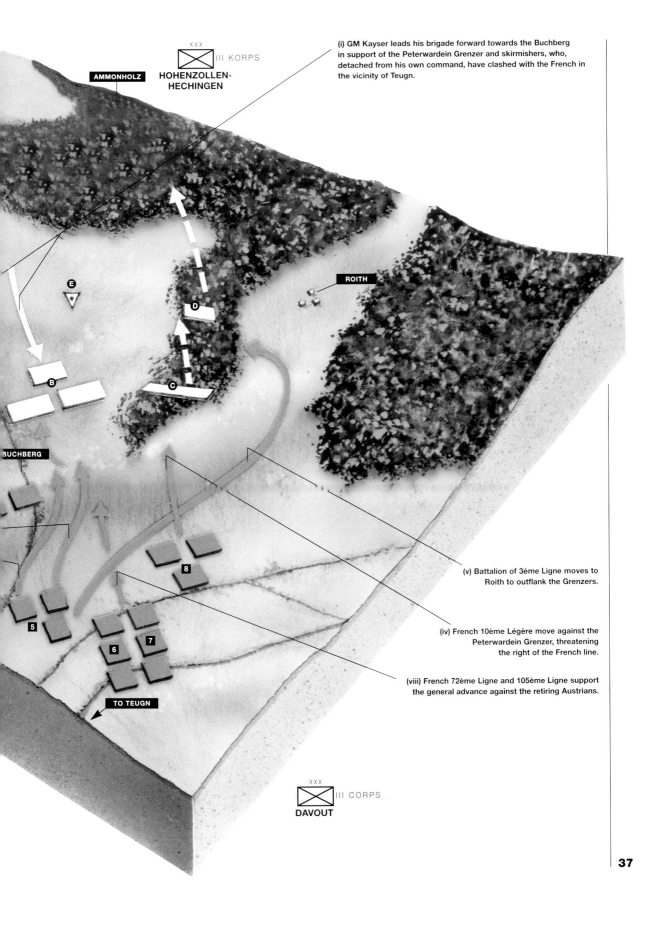

XXX
III KORPS
HOHENZOLLEN-HECHINGEN

AMMONHOLZ

(i) GM Kayser leads his brigade forward towards the Buchberg in support of the Peterwardein Grenzer and skirmishers, who, detached from his own command, have clashed with the French in the vicinity of Teugn.

ROITH

E

D

B

C

BUCHBERG

8

5

6

7

TO TEUGN

(v) Battalion of 3ème Ligne moves to Roith to outflank the Grenzers.

(iv) French 10ème Légère move against the Peterwardein Grenzer, threatening the right of the French line.

(viii) French 72ème Ligne and 105ème Ligne support the general advance against the retiring Austrians.

XXX
III CORPS
DAVOUT

RIGHT Generalleutnant Kronprinz
Ludwig, the 22-year-old son of the
Bavarian king, Maximilian Joseph.
The king had hoped that Napoleon
would give command of the corps
to Ludwig, but Napoleon refused
and handed overall command to
Lefebvre. Ludwig, who had little
military experience, and who had
strong feelings against Napoleon,
was given command of the 1st
Division of VII Corps. In the background is a scene from the battle
of Arnhofen on 19 April 1809.
(ASKB)

During the evening of 19 April Napoleon analysed the reports that had come in throughout the day from the numerous clashes. The French believed they had defeated a larger force at Teugn-Hausen than was actually the case. Napoleon looked forward to the following day with supreme confidence. Nothing he had heard gave him any reason to change his low opinion of the enemy. He felt the end of the campaign was near.

LIGHTNING STRIKES: NAPOLEON TURNS TO THE OFFENSIVE

On the evening of 19 April, as detailed earlier, Louis received the order from Charles to move V Korps through Rohr and Langquaid to join up with the main army. However, as Hiller had not yet closed up, Louis felt it unwise to move immediately. With enemy troops in some strength to his front, a premature move would leave the road to Landshut open.

About 9.00am on 20 April FML Hiller, riding ahead of his korps, reached Louis' headquarters. An order written at 7.30am arrived as the two korps commanders discussed the situation. In it Charles stated that he intended moving his army towards Regensburg, where he hoped to join up with Kolowrat's II Korps. As this move would leave Louis' right flank open, he was to pull back to Rottenburg while Hiller was to take up a position at Pfeffenhausen. Any detached brigades, including Thierry's, were to move back to Rohr. However, Hiller had come to a different conclusion from Charles and believed that French aggression was designed to shield their retreat back across the Danube at Kelheim. He decided against acting on Charles' orders, and instead stated that he would move VI Korps to Rohr, about 15km north of Pfeffenhausen. Although a little concerned by Hiller's decision, as the main body of the korps was still some way off, Louis held V Korps in its positions facing the Abens. But by now it was too late: Napoleon was about to launch his counter-attack.

General Oudinot, commander of II Corps, at the opening of the campaign. Massena and Oudinot were marching to Landshut to cut off any Austrian retreat as a result of Napoleon's advance at Abensberg. However, during the advance, Oudinot was ordered to move north and reinforce the left with two divisions. Oudinot became a marshal at the end of the campaign.

LEFT As Austrian III Korps moved towards Teugn, a brigade commanded by Thierry was detached to protect its rear. On 19 April Thierry encountered a body of Bavarians close to the village of Arnhofen. During the clash, the Austrian 4.Levenehr Dragoner initially drove back the Bavarian 1.Kronprinz Chevauxlegers but were themselves repelled by an artillery battery. Then, two squadrons of 1.Dragoner appeared, hit the Austrians in the flank and supported by the rallied Chevauxlegers drove them back. After some inconclusive infantry exchanges Thierry withdrew his command to Offenstetten. (Bayerische Verwaltung, Munich)

THE BATTLE OF ABENSBERG
20 APRIL 1809

apoleon arrived in Abensberg at 9.00am on the morning of 20 April, accompanied by Nansouty's 1st Heavy Cavalry Division, and prepared to open the offensive immediately. All available troops were directed on two lines of approach, initially on the strategically well- placed town of Rohr. Napoleon presumed that Davout's victory of the previous day would set the Austrian army in retreat. By pushing on Rohr, he would intercept them or, if not, at least push them back on Landshut, where they would find Massena waiting. The responsibility for the left line of advance, which would move on the line Offenstetten–Bachl–Rohr, was handed to the newly arrived Marshal Lannes. For this purpose a provisional corps was created: Morand's and Gudin's infantry Divisions from III Corps, two chasseurs à cheval regiments from Montbrun's Light Cavalry Division, Nansouty's heavy cavalry and Clément's cuirassier brigade from Saint Sulpice's Heavy Cavalry Division. At the same time, the Bavarian 1st Division was to advance from Abensberg, followed by the 3rd Division and Demont's Reserve Division, clearing the Austrians to their front before moving towards the Bachl–Rohr road. On the right Wrede's 2nd Bavarian Division was to move through Biburg and attempt to cut off any Austrian retreat from Rohr towards Landshut. They were to be supported by the Württembergers. Spread out in the path of this advance stood the

Three days after his arrival at the front, Napoleon was full of confidence and ready to unleash his army. With Davout's victory at Teugn-Hausen he expected the Austrians to be retreating. By pushing forward towards Rohr, he hoped to intercept them or push them back onto Massena, who was heading for Landshut. (ASKB)

On the morning of 20 April Napoleon made a stirring speech to the officers of Bavarian 1st and 3rd divisions at Abensberg. Recalling old animosities, Napoleon called on the Bavarians to "attack them [the Austrians] with the bayonet and destroy them!" The soldiers, suitably inspired, then received a double beer ration. (ASKB)

isolated commands of Thierry, Bianchi, Pfanzelter and Schustekh.

Thierry, who had just over three battalions of infantry, the 4. Levenehr-Dragoner and two 3pdr. guns, was concerned about his exposed position. When the first Bavarian units appeared opposite Offenstetten at about 10.00am, he informed Pfanzelter that he was about to retreat, and he appealed for support. Thierry fell back, but when he approached Bachl, there was no sign of Pfanzelter. GM Josef Pfanzelter, who had been detached from III Korps as it had moved on Hausen, had been left there in command of 1st Battalion of 9. Peterwardein Grenzer, two squadrons of 3. Erzherzog Ferdinand-Husaren and half a 3pdr. battery. Early in the morning his outposts had been put under pressure by the movement of Lannes' provisional corps. Then Pfanzelter had received an order from headquarters which stated that he and Thierry should march to rejoin III Korps. Therefore, as Lannes began to approach Bachl from the north, late in the morning, Pfanzelter marched off towards Langquaid without informing Thierry, but did send a message to FML Schustekh in Rohr. Attacked on their withdrawal by French cavalry, Pfanzelter lost two guns and two Grenzer companies were captured, but the rest made it safely to Langquaid and shortly afterwards rejoined III Korps' advance guard.

Thierry was now alone. He had not received the order to retire on Langquaid and with no obvious friendly forces in the vicinity, Thierry ordered his men to march on Rohr, using the woods to the west of the road to protect them from the attentions of the French cavalry. But the weary men, who had been pressed all day, finally broke and lost all order as they retreated on Rohr, where they began to arrive around 2.00pm.

THE AUSTRIANS ARE DRIVEN BACK

FML Schustekh had been detached from Louis' V Korps to hold Rohr with eight companies drawn from 7. Brod Grenzer and four squadrons of 8. Kienmayer-Husaren. He was aware that Thierry had been engaged with the enemy and was now retreating, and that Pfanzelter was fol-

lowing orders and falling back on Langquaid. Schustekh wanted to withdraw towards Pfeffenhausen but recognised the importance of his position in offering support to Thierry's retreating men. Forming his men on the hills behind the town, he saw Thierry's men approach, closely followed by French chasseurs à cheval. These in turn were followed by Saint Sulpice's cuirassiers and Morand's infantry. Hopelessly outnumbered, Schustekh's attempt to delay the pursuers failed. The French horsemen galloped on down the road leading to Rottenburg, creating mayhem among the retreating Austrians and their transport. While attempting to make a stand, the unfortunate Thierry and a large

The first phase of the Battle of Abensberg, 20 April 1809. The Bavarian 1st Division advance from Abensberg towards Offenstetten preceded by their Schützen and followed by the divisional artillery. Ahead of them was the unsupported Austrian brigade of GM Thierry.

ABOVE **A contemporary French illustration of the Battle of Abensberg. It is difficult to discover if this stylised view of the battle purports to show any specific incident. It is possibly the artist's confused rendition of a failed attempt by the Bavarians to cross the Abens at Siegenburg and the outflanking movement at Biburg. (ASKB)**

RIGHT **Archduke Louis (Erzherzog Ludwig), commander of V Korps. On 20 April Louis also commanded part of II Reserve Korps and had been ordered to move towards Siegenburg and oppose any aggressive movements by the Bavarians. When the French-Allied offensive began, he was driven back on Pfeffenhausen.**

LEFT **After the capture of Offenstetten and a farmstead close by, the Bavarians were attacked by two squadrons of 4. Levenehr-Dragoner. Although this illustration depicts the Dragoons attacking French troops, it is supposed to represent this incident, as the hastily formed Bavarian squares manage to drive off the attack. (ÖNB)**

number of men were captured. The French pursuit only halted when it ran into advanced units of VI Korps just outside Rottenburg between 4.00 and 5.00pm.

In the meantime, Bavarian II Division, supported by the Württembergers, had launched their attack and made contact with outposts of GM Bianchi's brigade of V Korps around Biburg. However, it was not until the early part of the afternoon that the Bavarians crossed the Abens in strength, at which point Bianchi pulled back and established himself in a good position with almost eight battalions, just over a squadron of cavalry and 11 guns. From here, Bianchi's men were able to repel all Bavarian attempts on the position until Louis issued an order at about 2.00pm for all front-line units to begin to withdraw as pressure increased. Bianchi fell back and joined the main body at Schweinbach. GM Radetzky, with the advance guard of V Korps, held a position east of Siegenberg, covering the withdrawal of the rest of V Korps until he was attacked by a Bavarian battalion and two Württemberg light battalions; then he too fell back along the Pfeffenhausen road, having delayed the pursuit long enough for the main body of the korps to pull back. The pursuit was finally abandoned for the night around Schweinbach. When Louis arrived in Pfeffenhausen that evening he found the town in great confusion. Not only were the men of V and II Reserve Korps in and around the town, but they had also been joined by some units from VI Korps and a great number of transport wagons which had arrived down the road from Rottenburg. Louis ordered the transport to move on to Landshut immediately.

HILLER HALTS THE FRENCH ADVANCE

Hiller, after his meeting with Louis earlier in the morning, had returned to the main body of VI Korps, which was resting about 3km north-west of Pfeffenhausen. About noon the column broke camp and marched through Pfeffenhausen on the road to Rohr. The march through Pfeffenhausen itself was delayed, as the town was already filling up with soldiers from V Corps and the roads were choked by transport columns coming from the opposite direction. These delays meant that the lead units of VI Korps arrived near Rottenburg at about the same time as the French who had been pursuing the Austrians from Rohr. Determined to halt any further French advance, Hiller moved his two leading brigades forward. The first moved up the right bank of the Grosse Laaber and took up a position at Rottenburg. The second brigade, with some cavalry, crossed to the left bank of the river and after a number of clashes successfully brought the French advance to a halt before withdrawing to Rottenburg itself. Now aware that the French opposite him were in some strength and that Louis had fallen back to Pfeffenhausen, Hiller removed his korps to a position on the Klein Laaber at Turkenfeld. Late that evening Hiller attempted to send a message to Charles, but the

GM Josef Graf Radetzky commanded a brigade of V Korps at the Battle of Abensberg. During V Korps' retreat, Radetzky commanded its rearguard and was most energetic in delaying the Bavarian-Württemberg advance. In later years, as field marshal, Radetzky led the Austrian army to victory over the Piedmontese at Custozza in 1848. (D. Hollins)

There were many separate engagements which made up the sweeping advance known as the Battle of Abensberg. This contemporary illustration carries the description 'Capturing a village on 20 April' and represents just one of them. (ASKB)

BATTLE OF ABENSBERG, 20 APRIL 1809

Napoleon launches his counter-offensive.

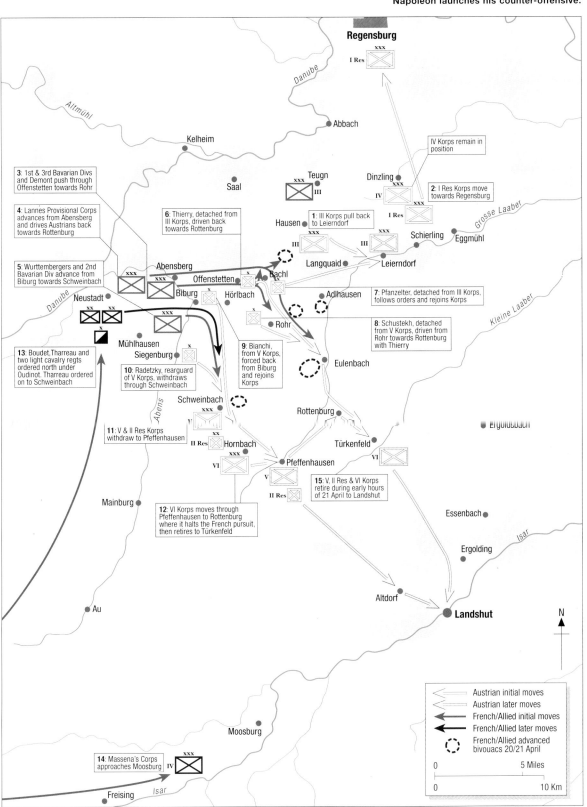

Regensburg

I Res

IV Korps remain in position

2: I Res Korps move towards Regensburg

Teugn
III

Abbach

Dinzling
IV

I Res

Saal

Kelheim

3: 1st & 3rd Bavarian Divs and Demont push through Offenstetten towards Rohr

6: Thierry, detached from III Korps, driven back towards Rottenburg

1: III Korps pull back to Leierndorf

Schierling

Eggmühl

Grosse Laaber

4: Lannes Provisional Corps advances from Abensberg and drives Austrians back towards Rottburg

Hausen
III

III

5: Wurttembergers and 2nd Bavarian Div advance from Biburg towards Schweinbach

Abensberg

Langquaid

Leierndorf

Offenstetten

Bachl
x

7: Pfanzelter, detached from III Korps, follows orders and rejoins Korps

Biburg
x

Hörlbach

Adlhausen

Danube

Neustadt

xx   xx
x

xxx

Rohr
x

Eulenbach

8: Schustekh, detached from V Korps, driven from Rohr towards Rottenburg with Thierry

13: Boudet, Tharreau and two light cavalry regts ordered north under Oudinot. Tharreau ordered on to Schweinbach

Mühlhausen

Siegenburg
x

9: Bianchi, from V Korps, forced back from Biburg and rejoins Korps

10: Radetzky, rearguard of V Korps, withdraws through Schweinbach

Schweinbach

Rottenburg

Ergoldsbach

Abens

V
xxx

11: V & II Res Korps withdraw to Pfeffenhausen

xx
II Res

Hornbach

Türkenfeld

VI

VI
xxx

12: VI Korps moves through Pfeffenhausen to Rottenburg where it halts the French pursuit, then retires to Türkenfeld

Mainburg

V

Pfeffenhausen

15: V, II Res & VI Korps retire during early hours of 21 April to Landshut

II Res

Essenbach

Ergolding

Isar

Au

Altdorf

Landshut

N

Moosburg

14: Massena's Corps approaches Moosburg

IV
xxx

Freising   Isar

	Austrian initial moves
	Austrian later moves
	French/Allied initial moves
	French/Allied later moves
	French/Allied advanced bivouacs 20/21 April

0   5 Miles

0   10 Km

45

FML Johann Freiherr Hiller had command of VI Corps in 1809. On 20 April, contrary to his orders, he was marching towards Rohr when he found himself against the advancing French. He made a stand with two brigades at Rottenburg and halted their pursuit. (D. Hollins)

messenger was unable to get through; Napoleon had driven a wedge through the two wings of Charles' army. Hiller was no longer under the notion that the French army was in retreat.

For the French, and their German allies, it had been a successful day at very low cost. Now, after another day exposed to the cold and wet, they formed into two main camps. The first spread across the area between Rohr and Rottenburg and the second around Schweinbach on the Pfeffenhausen road. Meanwhile, to the south, Massena had been driving his men onwards throughout 20 April. In response to Napoleon's communication of the previous day, Massena had ordered Tharreau's Division of II Corps to march towards the Abens to support the left wing of the army, along with two light cavalry regiments from Colbert's brigade of the same corps. Soon after, Oudinot was ordered to follow, taking with him Boudet's Division of IV Corps. By evening they were all at Neustädt, and soon after Tharreau was marching down the road towards Pfeffenhausen. The leading units of Massena's command pushed on and arrived before Moosberg that evening.

By the late evening of 20 April Napoleon had moved his headquarters to Rohr. Having studied all the day's reports, he had already determined his next moves. While he was not aware of the exact positions of the Austrian army, he was sure he had set the bulk of it in retreat; now he wanted to destroy it. He wrongly concluded that the resistance offered by the Austrians during the day had been to protect the retreat of the army defeated at Teugn-Hausen. Therefore, by driving on 21 April along the roads to Landshut, where he hoped Massena was positioned, he could complete the destruction of his enemy. Orders were sent to Davout, from whom Napoleon had heard little, informing him, confidently but erroneously, that he could only be facing a rearguard. Furthermore, Davout was told that a force commanded by Lefebvre (Demont's Division, Deroy's 3rd Bavarian Division and St. Germain's cuirassiers from Nansouty's Division) would move in the direction of Langquaid to drive away this rearguard and follow it on whatever route it took towards the Iser. Once this position was cleared, Davout was to take his two divisions and Boudet's, which had now arrived on the Abens, move to Regensburg and drive back the Austrians operating north of the Danube into Bohemia. Orders were also despatched that night for the two forces about Pfeffenhausen and Rottenburg to continue their pursuit of the Austrians towards Landshut.

THE SECOND BATTLE OF LANDSHUT, 21 APRIL 1809

Hiller and Louis began their retreat back to Landshut during the night of 20/21 April. As the French pursued, the cavalry of both sides clashed. This illustration shows chasseurs à cheval of Jacquinot's brigade engaging Austrian chevaulegers.

While Napoleon had been planning his moves for 21 April, Hiller and Louis had been considering their options. Both felt they could not successfully hold their positions against strong enemy pressure, so during the night their forces began to retire on Landshut. The first units of Louis' command arrived at the unfortified town at about 5.00am on 21 April. It was only five days since they had victoriously passed through it. However, when Louis and Hiller arrived this time, there were scenes of chaos on the narrow roads. The need to delay the advancing French was obvious.

The Spital bridge and the Lend bridge were each to be defended while preparations were made for the destruction of the bridges. Batteries were positioned on the heights of the Prielfeld, overlooking the river. Some of Louis' men were positioned on the high ground northeast of Altdorf, with outposts further out. The rest of his korps and Hiller's passed through the town, adding to its garrison or forming on the heights. Behind Louis' detachments a rearguard was formed by the third battalions of IR39 Duka and IR60 Gyulai of V Korps, drawn up in masses by the road at St. Nikolai, and by the 1st Battalion of IR49 Kerpen from VI Korps which held the other northern suburb of Seelingthal. However, at about 7.00am Hiller heard the disturbing news that a French force had crossed the Iser upstream at Moosberg. This was Massena. With a force of unknown strength marching against his flank, Hiller realised that it would now prove impossible to make a lengthy defence of the line of the Iser. North of Altdorf a fierce cavalry skirmish developed. While this action was taking place, Louis abandoned the positions

The town and environs of Landshut. Two battles were fought in this area, on 16 and 21 April 1809.

around Altdorf and retired on Landshut, crossed the river and moved onto the heights. The outnumbered Austrian cavalry then broke and also retreated to the town. With this the French and Allied cavalry swept forward. The advance, by the Bavarian cavalry brigades of Preysing and von Zandt, 11 squadrons of Württembergers, Jacquinot's two regiments of chasseurs à cheval and a body of French cuirassiers, was initially stalled by the fire of the infantry defending the suburbs. But having gained some breathing space for themselves, these men fell back onto the island of Zwischenbrücken.

FRENCH INFANTRY ASSAULT LANDSHUT

There had not been time to completely destroy the bridge over the northern arm of the Iser, so Hiller did not intend a particularly determined defence of this position. A short lull now descended, as the

The present-day bridge over the Iser at Landshut. As can be seen from the accompanying near-contemporary paintings, the view across the river has changed little over the intervening years.

French brought forward their infantry to take over the assault. The first of these units were the French 13ème Légère and 17ème Ligne from Morand's Division, along with two companies of light infantry from the Württemberg 3rd Brigade and a number of Bavarian battalions from Wrede's 2nd Division. The three Austrian battalions, with the addition of two companies of IR31 Benjowsky, opened a heavy fire from Zwischenbrücken on the advancing infantry and forced them to halt and engage in a firefight. As the French began to form an assault column to force the first bridge, Hiller ordered the defenders to retire over the

As the last of the Austrian rearguard entered Landshut, the bridge was set on fire, although the materials available were soaked through. Facing a storm of shot and shell, the grenadiers of 17ème Ligne were ordered across and succeeded in breaking through the gateway at the far end.

Napoleon's aide, General Mouton, was ordered to lead the storming of the bridge. Positioned at the head of the grenadiers, he is said to have led them forward shouting: "No firing! March!" In admiration, Napoleon is reputed to have joked: "My mouton [sheep] is a lion."

Spital bridge into Landshut, as there was now no longer time to save any more of the transport lying abandoned in the streets. As these men withdrew to the bridge, attempts were made to set it alight, but the rain which had been so prevalent over the previous days had soaked the materials placed on the wooden bridge and the flames only took hold reluctantly as the French stormed into Zwischenbrücken.

The position now confronting the French was a daunting one. At the far end of the slowly burning bridge was a large stone gateway with closed heavy wooden doors. The Austrian defenders fired down on it from both sides of the bridge and across it from the windows of the neighbouring buildings and from the large church close to the bridge. Napoleon, lacking knowledge of Massena's whereabouts, was determined to waste no more time. Calling for his aide, General Mouton, Napoleon ordered him to storm the bridge. Without hesitation, Mouton took up a position at the head of the grenadiers of 17ème Ligne and, reputedly shouting "No firing! March!" led them across the slowly burning bridge, assailed on all sides by shot and shell. Despite the mounting casualties, the grenadiers reached the barred gateway and the axe-wielding pioneers set to with a will and smashed their way through. The grenadiers burst into Landshut amid scenes of great confusion, and fought on through the narrow crowded streets. Immediately behind the grenadiers more men poured across the bridge. In the van came a body of Bavarians, a squadron of the 3. Leiningen-Chevaulegers and 7. Löwenstein infantry regiment, as well as the two companies of Württembergers and two battalions of 13ème Légère.

The Austrians in the town fought on. Men from the 6. Warasdin-St. Georg and 8 Gradiska Grenzer and infantry from IR31 Benjowsky, IR51 Spenyi and IR59 Jordis continued the struggle, but their time was running out. The French had also crossed at the Lend bridge, and the defenders were becoming surrounded. Before long many were captured, but a large part of the artillery escaped by the resolute actions of a battalion of IR14 Klebek. By their stout defence of the town's upper part, those who had fled back through the streets were given time to re-form on the high ground to the south. Landshut finally fell at about 1.00pm, and by then V Korps had received orders to retreat towards Vilsbiburg, on the road to Neumarkt. The anticipated arrival of Massena's force on the flank had taken place, and Hiller was determined to get his command away as intact as possible. By nightfall the main body of his command was encamped around Neumarkt.

Napoleon set up his headquarters in the castle at Landshut, while the main body of his army encamped in and around the town. In the course of the day the Austrians had lost about 8,000 men, dead, wounded and captured, along with 11 pieces of artillery, a pontoon train and vast amounts of transport and equipment. For the French-Allied soldiers and the good burghers of Landshut there was much profitable looting to be had from the abandoned wagons. But all was not as well as it seemed for Napoleon. Throughout the day a number of reports had been received from Davout who had been ordered to push on to Regensburg. In these reports Davout expressed the opinion that it was he who was facing the main Austrian army, not Napoleon. Unwilling to accept that he had misread the situation, Napoleon continued with his belief that the main army was before him and in retreat. However, during the evening of 21 April doubts began to enter his mind. Then, at about 2.00am on the morning of 22 April, an exhausted General Piré arrived in Landshut. Despatched by Davout at about 7.00pm, Piré informed Napoleon of what had developed throughout the day on the left-hand sector of the front line.

There was no longer any denying the situation, and Napoleon acted fast to retrieve what appeared to be an extremely dangerous position. The truth was that Regensburg had fallen, with its bridge intact, allowing Austrian troops to cross from the north bank of the Danube unopposed and link up with Archduke Charles and the main body of the army. Already they were engaged in battle with Davout and Lefebvre.

Once Mouton had broken into Landshut, he was swiftly followed by a squadron of Bavarian chevaulegers and 7. Löwenstein infantry. Inside the town the fighting was fierce and confused, but Hiller knew that Massena was about to outflank him and was determined to withdraw. (ASKB)

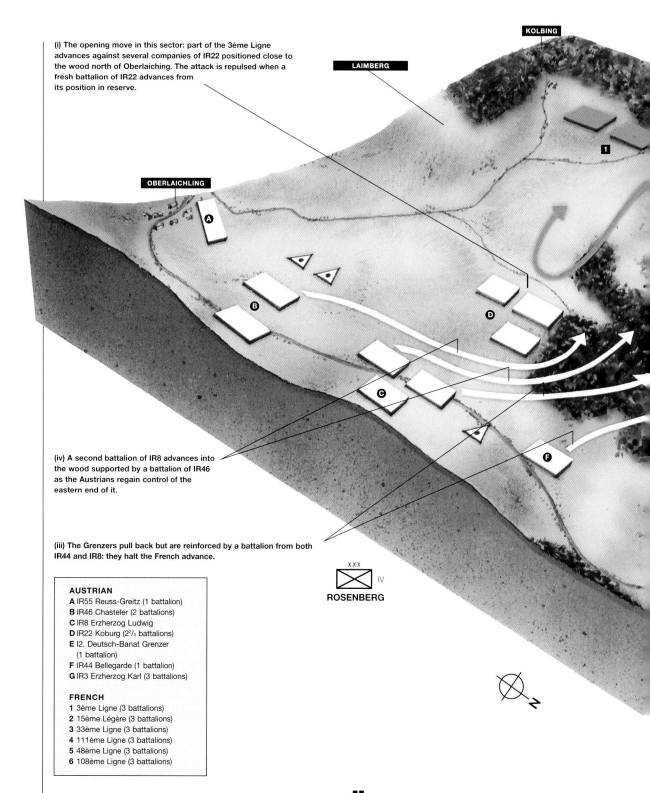

KOLBING

LAIMBERG

(i) The opening move in this sector: part of the 3ème Ligne advances against several companies of IR22 positioned close to the wood north of Oberlaiching. The attack is repulsed when a fresh battalion of IR22 advances from its position in reserve.

OBERLAICHLING

1

A

B

D

C

F

(iv) A second battalion of IR8 advances into the wood supported by a battalion of IR46 as the Austrians regain control of the eastern end of it.

(iii) The Grenzers pull back but are reinforced by a battalion from both IR44 and IR8: they halt the French advance.

xxx

IV

ROSENBERG

AUSTRIAN
A IR55 Reuss-Greitz (1 battalion)
B IR46 Chasteler (2 battalions)
C IR8 Erzherzog Ludwig
D IR22 Koburg (2²/₃ battalions)
E I2. Deutsch-Banat Grenzer
   (1 battalion)
F IR44 Bellegarde (1 battalion)
G IR3 Erzherzog Karl (3 battalions)

FRENCH
1 3ème Ligne (3 battalions)
2 15ème Légère (3 battalions)
3 33ème Ligne (3 battalions)
4 111ème Ligne (3 battalions)
5 48ème Ligne (3 battalions)
6 108ème Ligne (3 battalions)

BATTLE OF EGGMÜHL DAY 1 (21 APRIL 1809)

The French attempt to turn the right flank of Austrian IV Korps.

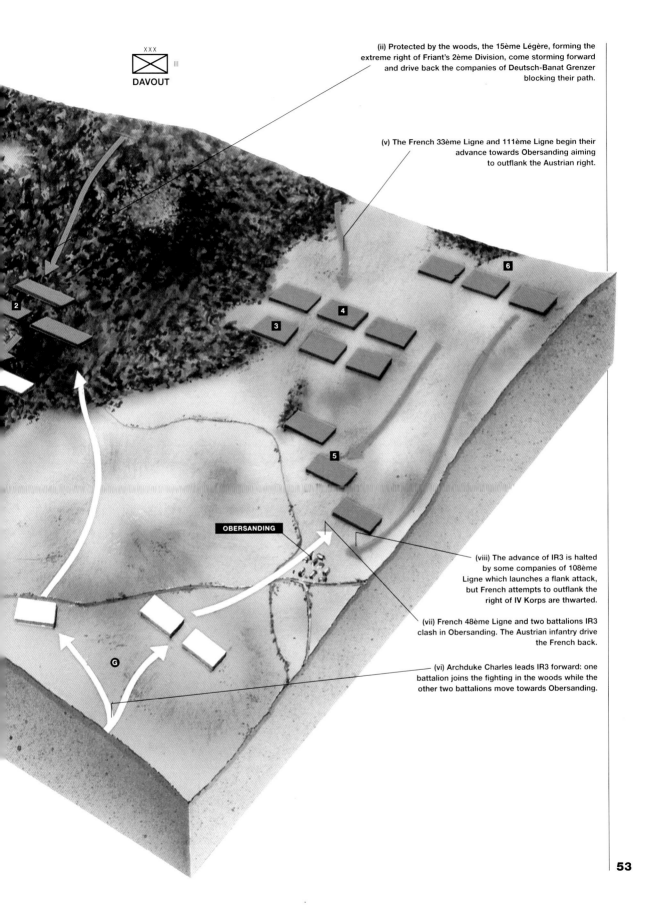

XXX
III
DAVOUT

(ii) Protected by the woods, the 15ème Légère, forming the extreme right of Friant's 2ème Division, come storming forward and drive back the companies of Deutsch-Banat Grenzer blocking their path.

(v) The French 33ème Ligne and 111ème Ligne begin their advance towards Obersanding aiming to outflank the Austrian right.

2

6

4

3

5

OBERSANDING

(viii) The advance of IR3 is halted by some companies of 108ème Ligne which launches a flank attack, but French attempts to outflank the right of IV Korps are thwarted.

(vii) French 48ème Ligne and two battalions IR3 clash in Obersanding. The Austrian infantry drive the French back.

G

(vi) Archduke Charles leads IR3 forward: one battalion joins the fighting in the woods while the other two battalions move towards Obersanding.

THE DELUGE: THE BATTLE OF EGGMÜHL, 21-22 APRIL 1809

REGENSBURG CAPTURED

ack at Austrian headquarters in Hausen on the morning of 20 April, the day after the battle of Teugn-Hausen, Charles was preparing for further action. In a report sent that day to Emperor Francis, he concluded with: "Your Majesty's troops have performed very bravely, but have also suffered heavily... I am again deploying the troops in battle order and awaiting further moves by the enemy." For this, Charles required the support of Kolowrat's II Korps, currently north of the Danube, outside Regensburg. The strength of the French garrison left behind in Regensburg was

GdK Johann Fürst Liechtenstein, commander of I Reserve Korps. Determined to capture Regensburg as quickly as possible, Charles ordered Liechtenstein to attack the city from the south on 20 April, while Kolowrat moved against it from the north. (D. Hollins)

The bridge at Regensburg. The 65ème Ligne surrendered Regensburg to Liechtenstein on the evening of 20 April. To the great relief of the Austrians, they found that the French garrison had been unable to destroy the strategically important bridge across the Danube.

unknown to Charles, and presuming it to be of some strength, he ordered Liechtenstein's command to attack the city from the south while Kolowrat operated against it from the north. However, as we have already seen, the garrison now consisted of only three hard-pressed battalions of the 65ème Ligne, who were running short of ammunition, but without this line of retreat open to him, Charles felt it unwise to initiate any aggressive moves with the recovering III Korps and IV Korps against an enemy of unknown strength between Teugn and Saal. Thus the order for a withdrawal to a more secure position.

In line with their orders, III Korps began to retire from the area around Hausen on the morning of 20 April. The main part of the korps crossed the Grosse Laaber river and deployed back from the river behind Ober and Nieder Leierndorf. That evening Pfanzelter's detachment, which had been posted in Bachl, struggled in, after surviving its clash with elements of Lannes' command, and joined the advance guard. Of Thierry, of course, there was no sign. IV Korps remained centred around Dünzling throughout the day, maintaining contact with III Korps. During 20 April Davout had moved St. Hilaire's Division through Hausen and made camp close by. Friant had his headquarters in Teugn and his division was encamped between there and Peising. Montbrun's Light Cavalry Division was also located around Peising. Otherwise there was little activity. Charles was under the impression that the French were in far greater strength than was the case, and he declined to attack until reinforced.

In the meantime, Liechtenstein marched on Regensburg, completing the encirclement of the city, and accepted its surrender at about 6.00pm. He then occupied it and discovered that the French had been unable to render the massive stone bridge unusable. Bellegarde's two korps on the north bank of the river resumed their operations north of the Danube.

DAVOUT PURSUES THE AUSTRIANS

On the evening of 20 April Napoleon had sent a message to Davout from Bachl. Having already decided to continue the pursuit of what he believed to be the main army towards Landshut, he merely instructed Davout to "advance anywhere there are enemy troops, to attack and destroy them". Spurred on by this, Davout took the decision to attack III Korps, which he had observed slowly withdrawing to Leierndorf. In the early hours of 21 April the French advance guard moved forward. Observing the beginning of this general advance against his position, Hohenzollern ordered his advance guard to fall back across the Grosse Laaber, destroying the bridges as they went. St. Hilaire's Division followed, turning to the east and marching along the north bank of the river. Friant's Division followed on behind St. Hilaire's men, before forming into line on their left flank and marching on a line through Schneidhart towards Paring. Directly in their path stood a mixed detachment from IV Korps. Orders were hurriedly despatched for GM Stutterheim to reinforce this detachment, but by the time he appeared, they had been forced back by Friant's skirmishers to Paring. Stutterheim was then entrusted with the task of protecting IV Korps' southern flank, which was pulling back towards the twin villages of Unter and Ober Laiching in light of this French movement. Stutterheim performed his task well and gained enough time for Rosenberg to redeploy IV Korps successfully.

Meanwhile, Austrian III Korps had been in action too. Following his orders from Napoleon issued during the evening of 20 April, Lefebvre had commenced his advance from Bachl at about 5.00am the following morning. Lefebvre's command now consisted of Demont's French Reserve Division. Deroy's Bavarian 3rd Division and St. Germain's 3ème and 12ème cuirassiers from Nansouty's Heavy Cavalry Division (approx. 13,500 men). With the approach of this force towards Langquaid and the build-up of Friant and St. Hilaire's men north of the Grosse Laaber, Hohenzollern ordered his korps to retire to a new position behind the Allerdorf stream, which ran into the Grosse Laaber on the south side of Schierling. The first line formed behind the stream, while the second was positioned a little further back, either side of Lindach. Demont's Division, which was leading Lefebvre's force, had attempted to attack across the river at Leierndorf, but finding the bridges destroyed and coming under shell fire, they were forced out of the village.

Marshal Lefebvre, Duc de Danzig, (1755-1820), commander of VII (Bavarian) Corps. On 21 April, after the dispersal of his corps during the Battle of Abensberg, Lefebvre followed Hohenzollern's retreat and moved against Schierling with a mixed Bavarian and French force.

CHARLES RE-FORMS THE ARMY

Charles, who had moved his headquarters to Alteglofsheim during the morning, had been preparing new orders for his army; these entailed a concentration between Eggmühl and Regensburg prior to launching an attack on 22 April. Then, shortly after the orders were despatched, the first news of the French advance was received, throwing his plans into disarray. In the meantime, Rosenberg sent in a message stating that he was falling back with IV Korps towards the Laichings. Hohenzollern advised Charles that he was falling back too, to the position south of Schierling, but before he received these messages, Charles' order for III Korps to retreat back through Schierling and Eggmühl to reassemble on the hills behind the Laichings had been despatched. A brigade was to be left at Lindach with some of the advance guard, and the rest of this force was to take up a position on the north bank of the Grosse Laaber, reaching out towards IV Korps. Rosenberg, who unknown to Charles was already pulling back his main body from Dünzling, was required to hold his position behind that village. Orders were also sent to Liechtenstein to move his command to a position around Wolkering, west of Alteglofsheim, from where he could support the presumed right flank of IV Korps. Drawn up to the rear in a supporting position were two regiments of kürassiere. Other troops were also ordered towards this area. The three battalions of IR3 Erzherzog Karl were placed in the villages of Haus, Mooshof and Höhenberg; close by were six grenadier battalions and two regiments of kürassiere. Between Haus and Alteglofsheim, behind the right wing, another six grenadier battalions and two regiments of kürassiere were formed. In all, Charles presumed that he had about 57,600 infantry, 8,100 cavalry and 202 guns positioned in a line which extended for some 15km from Wolkering in the north, through Ober and Unter Laiching, and across the Grosse Laaber to Lindach.

As we have seen, Rosenberg carried out the retirement of IV Korps from Dünzling without orders from Charles, selecting the Laichings as the most appropriate position in which to align his korps, having closed the gap between himself and III Korps, who were still on the far bank of the Grosse Laaber. Now IV Korps were moving to occupy the ground Charles had selected for III Korps, instead of the area between Dünzling and Thalmassing that Charles had intended for them.

Rosenberg's men moved into position. The right of the line was anchored on a large wood, then it ran south across the open hills to the village of Oberlaiching and on to Unterlaiching. The hills behind the two villages rose quite steeply, and although the position could be subject to enemy artillery fire from the edge of the woods to the west, it appeared to be the best in the locality for defence. To protect his right flank Rosenberg ordered seven companies of 12. Deutsch-Banat Grenzer into the woods on which the line was anchored, and he supported them with 1st Battalion IR44 Bellegarde and an artillery battery. On the open hills between the woods and Oberlaiching were positioned several more batteries and three regiments of infantry – IR8 Erzherzog Ludwig, IR22 Koburg and IR46 Chasteler, although a number of the battalions were held back in reserve, in case the French threatened the right through the woods. Oberlaiching and the hills behind Unterlaiching were occupied by Neustädter's brigade, IR9 Czartoryski and IR55 Reuss-Greitz. An artillery battery and two squadrons of 4. Vincent-Chevauleger joined this formation on the hill behind Unterlaiching. From the summit of the hill, the Deisenberg, the slope ran sharply down to the village through thick woodland. Three companies of IR44 Bellegarde were pushed forward to occupy the village, while the other three companies positioned themselves in the wood. From Unterlaiching towards Schierling the ground was open rolling countryside, but a hill positioned between the two villages hid Schierling from view. Therefore an artillery battery was moved forward to the crest of this hill. South of the artillery and east of Schierling four squadrons of 4. Vincent-Chevauleger and six squadrons of 10. Stipsicz-Husaren stood. The whole of this advanced position was screened by five companies of 12. Deutsch-Banat Grenzer and another squadron of the Hussars. Satisfied at last that his position now looked quite secure, Rosenberg was horrified when he looked over to his left and observed III Korps retiring from Schierling. He immediately sent a message to Hohenzollern asking him to remain in position to secure the left flank of his korps. In reply, Hohenzollern reported that he was in receipt of an order from Charles to withdraw to a new position; however, that position was already occupied by Rosenberg.

FML Fürst Rosenberg-Orsini, commander of IV Korps. As the French began to move on 21 April, Rosenberg decided to retire to a position at the twin Laiching villages. He anchored his left on Unterlaiching and the right on a wood north of Oberlaiching. (ÖNB)

OPENING CLASHES

With the withdrawal of III Korps, Lefebvre was able to continue his advance largely unopposed. Having repaired the bridges at Leierndorf, one of Demont's brigades crossed to the southern bank of the Grosse

Laaber and advanced towards Schierling. Demont's other brigade, Deroy's Bavarian Division with Seydewitz's cavalry, and St. Germain's cuirassier brigade marched along the northern bank in the same direction. Aware that the Austrians had left a rearguard in Schierling, Lefebvre ordered them cleared out. The Bavarian 7. leichte Infanterie-Bataillon Günther stormed into the village and cleared that part north of the river fairly easily, but they rashly continued to advance right through the village and up the hill in the direction of Unterlaiching. Blasted by the battery on the hill and assaulted by 4. Vincent-Chevauleger, the Bavarians fled back towards Schierling in great disorder, having suffered many casualties. Such was their condition that they were withdrawn from the battle. Another attempt was made, and this time the assault by 5. leichte-Infanterie-Bataillon Butler and a battalion from Demont's Division was successful. They pushed the Austrian defenders back to Lindach but were unable to establish themselves beyond the village. A half squadron of 4. Chevaulegers-Regiment Bubenhofen and a squadron of 2. Dragoner-Regiment Taxis were then despatched southwards in the direction of Landshut in an attempt to link up with Lannes. The brigade of French infantry that crossed the Grosse Laaber at Leierndorf advanced to the Allersdorf stream, south of Schierling, and also halted. At roughly the same time as the attacks were

ABOVE **View from the Austrian line on the high ground above Oberlaiching. Beyond the small house is the Laimberg, where St. Hilaire positioned some of his artillery when his division emerged from the woods on the skyline before moving to attack Unterlaiching, off to the left of the photo.**

going on against Schierling, St. Hilaire's Division emerged from the woods west of the village of Kolbing and deployed on both sides of the village facing IV Korps. Some of the division's artillery positioned itself slightly to the front, on the slopes of the Laimberg, a hill between Kolbing and Oberlaiching. To the left of St. Hilaire Friant's men extended northwards, so its left was on a line through the village of Dünzling towards Obersanding.

Montbrun, the commander of the light cavalry, had been positioned at Peising, about 5km north-east of Teugn and close to Abbach and the Regensburg–Abensberg road. From early in the morning Montbrun had been reporting to Davout signs of increased enemy activity. At around 11.00am Davout sent Napoleon a report of this activity and also stated that he understood Regensburg had been taken by the Austrians. Davout began to grow concerned for his exposed left flank; he had already informed Napoleon that he felt the whole enemy army stood before him. Napoleon, confident that he was pursuing the main army himself, felt it unnecessary to order any significant assistance to his rather concerned and isolated marshal. Meanwhile, to guard against any drive by the Austrians into his rear along the Abbach road, Davout ordered Boudet, who had been detached from IV Corps a few days earlier, to support Montbrun with his division. Then, having taken these steps for the security of his position, Davout determined to gain as much time as possible to enable assistance to arrive. Aware that the Austrians had halted their withdrawal and were making a stand around Unter and Ober Laiching, he hoped to be able to pin them there and occupy their attention.

The heavily wooded country which extended around the position was ideal terrain for the well-adapted French infantry skirmishing tactics, and although outnumbered, Davout felt certain he could use the country to his advantage and negate the Austrians' numerical advantage. In particular, the extensive wooded area north of the Austrian position, on the high ground between Oberlaiching and Obersanding, would be ideal to secure his left and threaten the Austrians, while his far right could be held by Lefebvre, secured on Schierling. Montbrun, who did not know that Rosenberg had withdrawn IV Korps until about 1.00pm, left detachments at Abbach and Peising before moving the rest of his command to Dünzling, where he took up a position behind Friant at about 3.30pm. By this time, isolated actions had developed all along the line; in no time these actions escalated into ferocious struggles.

THE BATTLE BEGINS

The attacks were instigated by the French and were largely uncoordinated. From the woods on the right of St. Hilaire's position an attack was launched against Unterlaiching by a voltigeur company of 10ème Légère and a battalion of 57ème Ligne. The three companies of IR44 Bellegarde defending the village were outnumbered by the advancing French but defended themselves well, supported by the artillery battery on the Deisenberg above. The French penetrated the village and even into the woods which clung to the slope behind, but unsupported in their attack, they were eventually pushed out of the trees, through the

LEFT **The Battle of Eggmühl (second day). The village and Schloss of Eggmühl are in the centre. The hills are rather dramatic, but Unterlaiching can be seen at the foot of one to the left of centre. Gudin is advancing to the right of Eggmühl, Morand is crossing the river, extreme right. Both are under fire from Bieber on the high ground. The French cavalry are beginning to form on the watermeadows. On the left the French and Bavarian infantry are attacking Unterlaiching. (ASKB)**

The villages of Ober and Unter Laiching. This is the view of St. Hilaire's men as they emerged from the woods to attack. Oberlaiching is on the left, while Unterlaiching and its wood are in the centre.

village and forced to fall back on their original positions. The battery on the hill south-west of Unterlaiching came under heavy counter-battery fire from Bavarian and French guns, but managed to hold on and was joined by a 12pdr. battery which prevented any French or Bavarian advance through this area.

On the left centre of St. Hilaire's position an attack rolled forward over the Laimberg towards Oberlaiching, but this was met by part of the 12. Deutsch-Banat Grenzer holding the right of the Austrian position. Aided by a detachment from IR9 Czartoryski and a squadron of cavalry, the Grenzers were able to thwart the attack and persuade the French against sending any more attacks in from that direction for the remainder of the day. An attack by part of 3ème Ligne against the right flank of some companies of IR22 Koburg who were positioned close to the wood north of Oberlaiching appeared to be about to bring success, but it stalled when a fresh battalion of the same regiment came forward from its position in reserve and forced the French back again.

The whole area of the front line from Schierling to Oberlaiching now resounded to the boom and crash of artillery, but no further infantry attacks were ordered in this sector of the battlefield for the rest of the day. However, in the woods the fighting continued as fierce as ever. On the extreme right of Friant's Division, and linking with the left of St. Hilaire's, the 15ème Légère came storming through the woods north of Oberlaiching and began pushing back the companies of 12. Deutsch-Banat Grenzer which had been placed within its confines. Forced out of the woods, they fell back towards the village of Obersanding until, reinforced by a battalion each from IR44 Bellegarde and IR8 Erzherzog Ludwig, they were able to retrace their steps and halt the advance of the 15ème Légère. However, neither side was able to gain ground against the other, and the fighting continued indecisively until Rosenberg, recognising the danger if the French succeeded in establishing a strong position on his right flank, ordered another battalion of IR8 Erzherzog Ludwig into the fray. These men advanced with tremendous determination and drove the French, who had also received reinforcements, back, until the impetus of their attack faltered too. Then as the leading men hesitated, it appeared that the Austrians would lose all the ground they had just gained, until a part of IR46 Chasteler reinforced them and they finally managed to secure their hold on the eastern part of the woods.

CHARLES REINFORCES THE FRONT LINE

General Friant, commander of an infantry division in Davout's corps. On the first day of the Battle of Eggmühl, Friant directed his men in an attempt to drive through the woods and turn Rosenberg's right at Obersanding. This attempt failed when Charles sent forward IR3 to intercept.

Archduke Charles was at Höhenberg, where he had been since about 12.00 noon. Analysing the reports that were coming in, he realised that he was under attack by a strong force behind which he presumed were more enemy formations. By about 1.45pm he felt that IV Korps would need to be reinforced if it was to hold its position. Charles therefore sent a message to Liechtenstein, urging him to advance in support, but he was behind schedule and his command was not able to complete their assembly until late in the afternoon. The only troops close at hand in the northern sector were two squadrons of kürassiere drawn up to the west of Thalmassing. Charles' immediate concern was the threat that the French might force their way through his line at Ober and Unter Sanding and cut the important Eggmühl–Regensburg road. To prevent this, he decided to distribute III Korps to strengthen the line held by IV Korps. As it will be remembered, III Korps were already ordered back through Eggmühl. They had left their advance guard, two battalions of 9. Peterwardein Grenzers, four squadrons of 3. Erzherzog Ferdinand-Husaren and a cavalry battery of 6pdrs around Lindach, and GM Bieber's brigade had also been left on the southern bank of the Grosse Laaber closer to Eggmühl. During this move, Hohenzollern had received reports, presumably from Rosenberg, of the situation confronting IV Korps. In accordance with these reports, it appears that Hohenzollern intended forming his men to the right of IV Korps, but as he marched through Eggmühl, an aide arrived from Charles informing him that one of his brigades was required to march to Haus castle, close to Neueglofsheim. No sooner had GM Alois Liechtenstein's brigade of six battalions, an artillery battery and the divisional commander FML St. Julian marched off to the north, than another aide galloped up. He instructed Hohenzollern that he was to hand over another brigade and the battalion of the Erzherzog Karl Legion to march to the high ground behind Unterlaiching to support the left of IV Korps. As GM Kayser's brigade marched off, the bemused and angry commander of III Korps found himself with nothing but four squadrons of 3. Erzherzog Ferdinand-Husaren under his direct command. Then, at 4.00pm, Charles wrote to FZM Kolowrat of II Korps urging him to cross the Danube, making all speed, for it appeared to all at Austrian headquarters that the decisive battle was about to be fought. Charles then personally led forward the three battalions of IR3 Erzherzog Karl to the right of IV Korps. One battalion entered the woods north of Oberlaiching, while the other two opposed the units of Friant's Division that were attacking towards Obersanding, hoping to turn the Austrian right. The French attack was led by 33ème Ligne and supported by 111ème Ligne but it was the 48ème Ligne that forced their way into Obersanding. Unfortunately for them, at the same time, the two battalions of IR3 Erzherzog Karl arrived and pushed the French out again at the point of the bayonet. The Austrians, continuing their advance and pushing the French back, were themselves attacked in the right flank by some companies of 108ème Ligne and were forced to retire back to the village. The French withdrew to the woods west of Obersanding, from where they had debouched. Charles, now in the front line and assured that IV Korps' position was secure, ordered a halt to any further attacks that night since darkness was approaching. The bulk of the fighting throughout the day, through Paring to the Laichings, had been borne by Rosenberg's IV Korps, supported in the latter stages of the day by IR3 Erzherzog Karl, detached from V Korps. It appears that IV Korps sustained some 3,300 casualties that day, while the total French and Allied casualties were probably in the region of 1,900.

EVENING 21 APRIL 1809

Charles' Plans

The evening of 21 April was very cold and frosty and the soldiers settled down as best they could. When calm eventually descended on the battlefield, Davout wrote again to Napoleon, at about 7.00pm. This was the message carried by General Piré which reached Landshut at about 2.00am the following morning. Piré advised Napoleon that Davout was facing the main concentration of Charles' army and that Davout's left was dangerously threatened. He added that Davout felt unable to attack again as his men were low on ammunition. Finally he requested orders from Napoleon as to what was required of him. Back in the French camp that evening, Davout was reassured by the news that Oudinot, with Tharreau's Division, was now under his command, and Davout ordered him up to Langquaid. He learned later still that the infantry of the Bavarian 1st Division positioned at Rottenburg was also placed at his disposal.

GM Peter Vécsey, commander of the advance guard division of II Korps. Vécsey, a very able and independent leader, had been detached from II Korps since the beginning of the campaign. On 22 April he was appointed to provide the advance guards for the 1st and 2nd columns. (ÖNB)

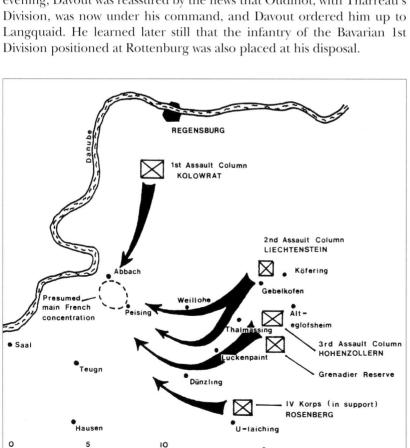

Charles' plan for 22 April 1809. Believing that the French were now concentrated on the hills between Abbach and Peising, Charles formed his army into three assault columns; these were supported by Rosenberg's korps. The attack was timed for 2.00pm, but by then the situation had dramatically changed.

GD Vandamme, commander of VIII (Württemberg) Corps. Having taken the decision to march north, Napoleon selected the Württemberg light troops to form the advance guard of the whole force. Their performance was exemplary. (P. Haythornthwaite)

When the day's fighting had died down, Charles issued orders for the overnight encampments of his army. Bieber's brigade and the advance guard of III Korps remained in their positions and were subordinated to the command of Rosenberg's IV Korps. The rest of III Korps were withdrawn from the front line and ordered to reassemble between Köfering and Alteglofsheim. Davout, reporting to Napoleon, described the Austrian camp fires sweeping around his position in an arc from Abbach to Lindach. Charles then returned to Alteglofsheim to consider his orders for the following day.

On the evening of 21 April Charles received his first news concerning the fate of the left wing of the army under Louis and Hiller. The reports were short on detail, however, and they did not mention the presence of Napoleon, who Charles had presumed was with the force opposing him. Therefore he believed Hiller would be strong enough to hold the line of the Iser at Landshut. With these French forces tied down, Charles felt he could bring enough strength to bear against the French opposing him and achieve a successful outcome. Having considered all the information they had to hand, Austrian headquarters wrongly concluded that the main concentration of the French was on the hills in the Abbach–Peising area. Accordingly, the plan for the following day, Saturday 22 April, was for a major thrust through Abbach towards Regensburg. The orders designated that three columns would carry out the main attack.

The 1st assault column, formed by II Korps with part of Vécsey's brigade as advance guard, was to march towards but bypass the town of Abbach. Due to the exertions II Korps had been forced to make, marching through the night, the general assault of the army was timed for 2.00pm to allow them an opportunity for rest. Kolowrat now had about 20,700 infantry, 2,630 cavalry and 71 guns. In addition, he was to destroy the Danube bridges as far downstream as Passau. The news that Hiller had fallen back to Landshut effectively ended that route as a line of communication and now the line would be taken across the Danube at Regensburg and back through Bohemia.

The 2nd assault column was formed by the infantry of Liechtenstein's command, with the addition of the remainder of Vécsey's brigade as advance guard. At 1.00pm they were to advance from their positions around Gebelkofen to Weillohe, with the advance guard extending to Luckenpaint. Liechtenstein now commanded some 10,500 infantry, 650 cavalry and 16 guns.

The 3rd assault column was formed mainly from III Korps, less those troops detached to IV Korps, but with the addition of the three battalions of IR3 Erzherzog Karl. This column, with 14,640 infantry, 500 cavalry and 69 guns, was to march from Castle Haus, near Neueglofsheim, at 12.00noon towards Peising via Luckenpaint and Dünzling. The orders for both the second and third columns specified that they were advancing against the 'right' of the French, confirming the Austrian belief that the French were about to strike north.

Rosenberg, with IV Korps, was to remain in position around the Laichings and attempt to occupy fully the attention of the French and their Allies while the main attack gathered momentum. Then, when the advance had reached a line with Thalmassing, he was to advance westwards from his position, aligning himself with the 3rd assault column but be ready to swing to his right if the enemy attempted to get between the two thrusts. Rosenberg had about 11,300 infantry, 1,950 cavalry and 56 guns.

The force left on the south bank of the Grosse Laaber, Bieber's brigade and the advance guard of III Korps, were to take orders from IV Korps, cross the river and guard the bridge at Eggmühl. This was believed to be the only crossing point in the area and was now defended by 4,300 infantry, 500 cavalry and 14 guns.

A reserve of grenadiers and kürassiere was also prepared. The grenadiers were to be held in their overnight positions at Haus and Mooshof and be prepared to attack the French head on should they force their way in between the 3rd assault column and IV Korps. The reserve numbered 11,500 men and 16 guns. Two kürassiere regiments, which had spent the night at Obertraubling, were to move up to Thalmassing, while the other four remained in position at Köfering. To this cavalry force of 4,100 men and 24 guns Archduke Charles attached himself. Bellegarde, with I Korps, remained on the north bank of the Danube and was not to be a part of the attack.

As a result of these dispositions, Charles' army of 83,300 men and 166 guns was to have: a left flank guard of 4,800 men at Eggmühl, on the road to Landshut; 13,250 men holding the line between the Sanding and Laiching villages; a reserve of 15,600 men; and a main assault group on the right of 49,670 men directed towards Abbach and Peising. Unfortunately for the Austrians they had misread the situation: against this main group there was but a scattering of men detached from Montbrun's force. The real danger was coming from the south.

Napoleon Realigns his Army

When General Piré arrived in Landshut and gave his report Napoleon finally recognised his error and immediately began to issue orders to send help to Davout. First Vandamme was ordered to lead an advance guard formed of the four Württemberg light battalions and part of their cavalry and march north to Ergoldsbach, 19km south of Eggmühl. 1. Fußjäger-Bataillon König moved into the town at about 7.00am and took the Austrian hussar piquet completely by surprise; only a handful escaped to warn of this movement. One Württemberg cavalry regiment was to patrol towards Straubing while the rest were to prepare to march and then join up with the advance guard. St. Sulpice was ordered to reach Ergoldbach by 6.00am. The head of Gudin's Division was to be at the same town by

Marshal Massena. Aware of the danger confronting Davout, Napoleon immediately altered his axis of advance and instructed Massena to lead his command of almost 30,000 men towards Eggmühl. He was preceded by Marshal Lannes' column.

9.00am, with Morand's following close behind. Also joining the advance north were two divisions of Nansouty's heavy cavalry, two regiments detached from Marulaz's light cavalry and six squadrons of Bavarian cavalry. This force amounted to about 20,000 infantry and almost 9,000 cavalry. The command of this scratch force was handed to Lannes.

Having now made his decision to change the axis of his advance Napoleon next ordered Massena to have his three divisions of infantry (about 26,100 men) and d'Espagne's Cuirassier (about 3,100 men) formed between Landshut and Ergolding ready to march north at 6.00am. They were joined by a light cavalry regiment from Colbert's brigade. The force Napoleon now had marching north totalled about 46,100 infantry, 13,000 cavalry and 116 guns. At 4.00am he wrote to Davout informing him that he intended to arrive before Eggmühl by midday and would commence his attack at 3.00pm. Napoleon added: "I am resolved today or at the latest tomorrow to annihilate the army of Archduke Charles." Before attaching himself to Massena's corps, Napoleon handed the pursuit of Hiller's wing of the army to Marshal Bessières. The force detailed was the main part of Marulaz's Light Cavalry Division (about 1,800 men), part of Jacquinot's cavalry brigade (900 men), Wrede's 2nd Bavarian Division (7,800 infantry, 230 cavalry and 18 guns) and Mollitor's Division of IV Corps (7,100 infantry and 12 guns).

The Battle of Eggmühl (second day). Beyond the Bavarian staff group in the left foreground is the village of Unterlaiching, with the wood behind. Austrian prisoners of IR44 are being escorted away from the village. On the far right there is a cavalry action, presumably the charge by Seydewitz against the Vorberg. (ASKB)

BATTLE OF EGGMÜHL, 22 APRIL 1809 (DAY 2)

The dawn of 22 April saw the whole valley of the Grosse Laaber covered by a thick blanket of fog. Neither side had any view of their opponents until the sun finally broke through, at about 8.00am. While the Austrian army shook itself into order for the escalation of the previous day's battle, Rosenberg, facing the open ground north of Schierling, began to grow concerned at the lack of activity shown by the French and Allied troops in this area. He could observe the men cooking and a large force of unsaddled cavalry, and to Rosenberg it seemed that they were awaiting other developments. Fearing an attack would eventually emerge from the direction of Schierling, he reoccupied the position on the hill south-west of Unterlaiching by sending forward two battalions of IR9 Czartoryski and two batteries. Then he wrote to Charles, suggesting that due to the presence of enemy cavalry on this flank it would be advantageous to deploy four regiments of kürassiere on the left wing.

NAPOLEON ATTACKS BUCHHAUSEN

By late morning Rosenberg received a report that enemy cavalry had been seen in Ergoldsbach around dawn, and were proceeding northwards towards Eggmühl. Bieber's brigade crossed to the north bank of the Grosse Laaber, as instructed, but Vukassovich kept his

The approach to Buchhausen. The village was defended by a detachment of the Peterwardein Grenzer. The Württemberg König Jäger stormed into the village while the rest of their brigade advanced either side. The Grenzer were driven out.
(D. Wright)

66

General Morand, commander of the 1st Division of Davout's III Corps. Separated from their parent corps since Teugn-Hausen, Morand's men were now attached to Lannes Provisional Corps. With Gudin's Division they were to find a way over the river towards Rogging.

advance guard – two weakened battalions of 9. Peterwardein Grenzer, four squadrons of 3. Erzherzog Ferdinand-Husaren and a cavalry artillery battery – on the hills around Lindach; a detachment of Grenzer was positioned further south, at Buchhausen. Between 1.00 and 2.00pm the advanced units of the French-Allied force from Landshut approached the village. Immediately the Württembergers stormed forward on either side of the village, while the König Jäger, leading the way, charged into the village. The heavily outnumbered Grenzer detachment fell back before this onslaught, and after a burst of counter-battery fire and some cavalry skirmishes, Vukassovich ordered his detachment back over the river, covered by his hussars. Once across the river, the Grenzer prepared to defend the bridge and occupy the village of Eggmühl itself. The battery moved just beyond the village, to the foot of the Bettelberg, the hill above the hamlet of Kraxenhofen, where the hussars rejoined them. Bieber's brigade moved eastwards onto the high ground overlooking the Grosse Laaber, occupying the area towards

ORDER OF BATTLE
Eggmühl, 22 April 1809 (day 2)

In constructing this order of battle, I have attempted to reflect the state of the army as it appeared at the battle, taking into account the numerous detachments made earlier in the campaign and making allowances for casualties suffered prior to 22 April.

AUSTRIAN ARMY

IV KORPS
Commander: FML ROSENBERG
Total strength approx. 11,300 infantry, 1,950 cavalry, 62 guns.

DIVISION: FML Somariva
Brigade: GM Stutterheim
12 Deutsch-Banat Grenzer (2 Bat.)
4 Vincent-Chevaulegers (8 sqns)
Grenz brigade battery (8 x 3pdr.)

Brigade: GM Radivojevich
10 Stipsicz-Husaren (7 sqns)
Cavalry battery
   (4 x 6pdr. and 2 x 7pdr. howitzers)

DIVISION: FML Dedovich
Position battery
   (4 x 6pdr. and 2 x 7pdr. howitzers)

Brigade: GM Grill
IR8 Erzherzog Ludwig (3 Bat.)
IR22 Koburg (2 and 2/3 Bat. [16 coys])
Brigade battery (8 x 6pdr.)

Brigade: GM Neustädter
IR9 Czartoryski (2 Bat.)
IR55 Reuss-Greitz (2 Bat.)
Brigade battery (8 x 6pdr.)

DIVISION: FML Hohenlohe

Brigade: GM Riese
IR44 Bellegarde (2 Bat.)
IR46 Chasteler (2 Bat.)
Brigade battery (8 x 6pdr.)

Reserve Artillery
Position battery
   (4 x 12pdr. and 2 x 7pdr. howitzers)
Position battery
   (4 x 12pdr. and 2 x 7pdr. howitzers)
Cavalry battery
   (4 x 6pdr. and 2 x 7pdr. howitzers)

Detached From III KORPS
Total strength approx. 4,300 infantry, 500 cavalry, 14 guns

Advance Guard: FML Vukassovich
9. Peterwardein Grenzer (1 and 2/3 Bat. [10 coys])
3. Erzherzog Ferdinand-Husaren (4 sqns)

Cavalry battery
   (4 x 6pdr. and 2 x 7pdr. howitzers)

Brigade: GM Bieber
IR20 Kaunitz (2 and 2/3 Bat. [16 coys])
IR38 Württemberg (2 Bat. [12 coys])
Brigade battery (8 x 6pdr.)

BATTLE OF EGGMÜHL (DAY 2), 22 APRIL 1809

Rosenberg, forming the rearguard of the Austrian army, attempts to delay the advance of the French-Allied forces.

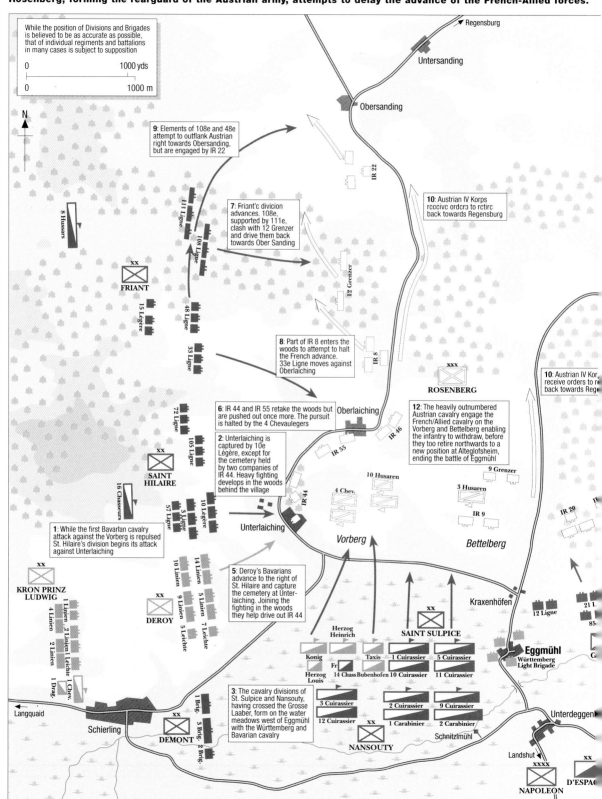

While the position of Divisions and Brigades is believed to be as accurate as possible, that of individual regiments and battalions in many cases is subject to supposition

0	1000 yds
0	1000 m

N

→ Regensburg

Untersanding

Obersanding

9: Elements of 108e and 48e attempt to outflank Austrian right towards Obersanding, but are engaged by IR 22

IR 22

10: Austrian IV Korps receive orders to retire back towards Regensburg

111 Ligne

7: Friant's division advances. 108e, supported by 111e, clash with 12 Grenzer and drive them back towards Ober Sanding

108 Ligne

8 Hussars

XX
FRIANT

12 Grenzer

15 Légère

48 Ligne

33 Ligne

8: Part of IR 8 enters the woods to attempt to halt the French advance. 33e Ligne moves against Oberlaiching

IR 8

XXX
ROSENBERG

10: Austrian IV Kor receive orders to r back towards Reg

72 Ligne

105 Ligne

6: IR 44 and IR 55 retake the woods but are pushed out once more. The pursuit is halted by the 4 Chevaulegers

Oberlaiching

IR 46

12: The heavily outnumbered Austrian cavalry engage the French/Allied cavalry on the Vorberg and Bettelberg enabling the infantry to withdraw, before they too retire northwards to a new position at Alteglofsheim, ending the battle of Eggmühl

2: Unterlaiching is captured by 10e Légère, except for the cemetery held by two companies of IR 44. Heavy fighting develops in the woods behind the village

IR 55

9 Grenzer

XX
SAINT HILAIRE

16 Chasseurs

57 Ligne

3 Ligne

10 Légère

IR 44

10 Husaren

4 Chev.

3 Husaren

IR 9

IR 20

Unterlaiching

Vorberg

Bettelberg

1: While the first Bavarian cavalry attack against the Vorberg is repulsed St. Hilaire's division begins its attack against Unterlaiching

XX
KRON PRINZ LUDWIG

14 Linien

10 Linien

5 Linien

9 Linien

7 Linien

XX
DEROY

5 Leichte

5: Deroy's Bavarians advance to the right of St. Hilaire and capture the cemetery at Unter-laiching. Joining the fighting in the woods they help drive out IR 44

Kraxenhöfen

12 Ligne

21 L

85

1 Linien

2 Linien

4 Linien

Leichte

Chev.

2 Linien

Herzog Heinrich

XX
SAINT SULPICE

Württemberg Light Brigade

Eggmühl
Württemberg

G

1 Dreg.

Konig

Fr

Taxis

1 Cuirassier

5 Cuirassier

Herzog Louis

14 Chass

Bubenhofen

10 Cuirassier

11 Cuirassier

3: The cavalry divisions of St. Sulpice and Nansouty, having crossed the Grosse Laaber, form on the water meadows west of Eggmühl with the Württemberg and Bavarian cavalry

3 Cuirassier

2 Cuirassier

9 Cuirassier

12 Cuirassier

XX
NANSOUTY

1 Carabinier

2 Carabinier

Unterdeggen

Schnitzlmühl

← Langquaid

XX
DEMONT

3 Brig.

2 Brig.

Landshut ◀

XXXX
D'ESPAG

Schierling

NANSOUTY

XXXX
NAPOLEON

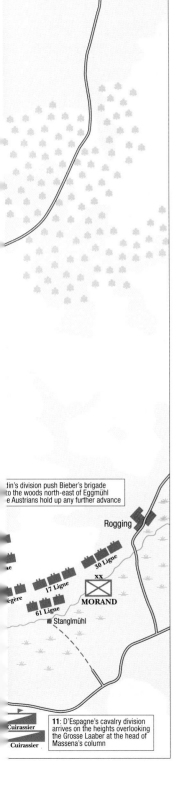

On map (left side):
Regensburg

...lin's division push Bieber's brigade
...to the woods north-east of Eggmühl
...e Austrians hold up any further advance

Rogging

30 Ligne
17 Ligne
61 Ligne
...égère
MORAND
Stanglmühl

Cuirassier
Cuirassier

11: D'Espagne's cavalry division
arrives on the heights overlooking
the Grosse Laaber at the head of
Massena's column

FRENCH/ALLIED ARMY

(Forces attacking from west of Eggmühl)

III CORPS
COMMANDER: MARÉCHAL DAVOUT
Total strength approx.19,000 infantry, 1,500
    cavalry, 23 guns

**2ème DIVISION: Général de Division
(GD) Friant**

Brigade: Général de Brigade (GB) Gilly
15ème Légère (3 Bat.)
33ème Ligne (3 Bat.)

Brigade: GB Grandeau
108ème Ligne (3 Bat.)
111ème Ligne (3 Bat.)

Brigade: GB Barbanègre
48ème Ligne (3 Bat.)

Foot battery (6 x 8pdr. and 2 x 6pdr.)

4ème DIVISION: GD Saint Hilaire
Brigade: GB Lorencez
10ème Légère (3 Bat.)
3ème Ligne (3 Bat.)
57ème Ligne (3 Bat.)

Brigade: GB Destabenrath
72ème Ligne (3 Bat.)
105ème Ligne (3 Bat.)

Foot battery
(6 x 8pdr. and 2 x 6pdr. howitzers)
Horse battery (5 x 6pdr. and 2 x 4pdr.)

**Cavalerie Légère Division:
GD Montbrun**

Brigade: GB Piré
8ème Hussards
16ème Chasseurs à cheval

VII (Bavarian) CORPS
COMMANDER: MARÉCHAL LEFÈBVRE
Total strength approx. 17,250 infantry,
    1,800 cavalry, 36 guns

**1. DIVISION: Generalleutnant (GL)
Kronprinz Ludwig**

**1. Brigade: Generalmajor (GM) Von
Rechberg**
1. Linien-Infanterie-Leibregiment (2 Bat.)
2. Linien-Infanterie-Regiment Kronprinz
(2 Bat.)
1. leichte Infanterie-Bataillon Habermann (1
Bat.)

2. Brigade: GM von Stengel
2. Linien-Infanterie-Regiment Herzog Pius (2
Bat.)
4. Linien-Infanterie-Regiment (2 Bat.)

Kavalleriebrigade: Oberst Vieregg
1. Dragoner-Regiment (2 sqns)
1. Chevaulegers-Regiment Kronprinz
(4 sqns)

Line battery (4 x 6pdr. and 2 x howitzers)
Line battery (4 x 6pdr. and 2 x howitzers)
Light battery (4 x 6pdr. and 2 x howitzers)

**3. DIVISION:
GL von Deroy**

1. Brigade: GM von Vicenti
9. Linien-Infanterie-Regiment Prinz
Yseinburg (2 Bat.)
10. Linien-Infanterie-Regiment Juncker
(2 Bat.)
5. leichte Infanterie-Bataillon Butler (1 Bat.)

2. Brigade: GM von Siebein
5. Linien-Infanterie-Regiment Preysing
(2 Bat.)
14. Linien-Infanterie-Regiment (2 Bat.)
7. leichte Infanterie-Bataillon Günther
(1 Bat.)

Kavalleriebrigade: GM von Seydewitz
2. Dragoner-Regiment Taxis (4 sqns)
4. Chevaulegers-Regiment Bubenhofen
(4 sqns)

Line battery (4 x 6pdr. and 2 x howitzers)
Line battery (4 x 6pdr. and 2 x howitzers)
Light battery (4 x 6pdr. and 2 x howitzers)

Temporarily Attached to VII Corps
RÉSERVE DIVISION: GD Demont

1ère Brigade
17ème Ligne (1 Bat.)
30ème Ligne (1 Bat.)
61ème Ligne (1 Bat.)
65ème Ligne (1 Bat.)

2ème Brigade
33ème Ligne (1 Bat.)
111ème Ligne (1 Bat.)

3ème Brigade
7ème Légère (1 Bat.)
12ème Ligne (1 Bat.)
21ème Ligne (1 Bat.)
85ème Ligne (1 Bat.)

(Forces attacking from south of
Eggmühl)
**COMMANDER IN CHIEF:
L'EMPEREUR NAPOLÉON**
Combined strength of Lannes and Massena
approx. 46,100 infantry, 12,810 cavalry,
116 guns

**PROVISIONAL CORPS
COMMANDER: MARÉCHAL LANNES**

Total strength approx. 20,000 infantry,
9,010 cavalry, 48 guns
Detached from **VIII (Württemberg)
CORPS**

3. (leichte) Brigade: GM von Hügel
1. Fußjäger-Bataillon König (1 Bat.)
2. Fußjäger-Bataillon von Neuffer (1 Bat.)
1. leichte Infanterie-Bataillon von Wolff
(1 Bat.)
2. leichte Infanterie-Bataillon von Brüsselle
(1 Bat.)

**KAVALLERIEDIVISION:
GL von Wöllwarth**

1. Brigade: GM von Röder
Chevaulegers-Regiment Herzog Heinrich
(4 sqns)

2. Brigade: GM von Stettner
Jäger-Regiment zu Pferd Herzog Louis
(2 sqns)
Jäger-Regiment zu Pferd König (4 sqns)

Horse battery
(4 x 6pdr. and 2 x 7pdr. howitzers)
Horse battery
(4 x 6pdr. and 2 x 7pdr. howitzers)

Detached from **CAVALERIE LÉGÈRE
DIVISION: GB Marulaz**
14ème Chasseurs à cheval (3 sqns)
Baden Leichte Dragoner-Regiment (4 sqns)

Detached from **III CORPS**
1ère DIVISION: GD Morand

Brigade: GB Lacour
13ème Légère (3 Bat.)
17ème Ligne (3 Bat.)
30ème Ligne (3 Bat.)

Brigade: GB l'Huiller
61ème Ligne (3 Bat.)

Foot battery (6 x 8pdr. and 2 x 6pdr.)
Horse battery (4 x 4pdr.)

3ème DIVISION: GD Gudin

Brigade: GB Petit
7ème Légère (2 Bat.)

Brigade: GB Boyer
12ème Ligne (2 Bat.)
21ème Ligne (3 Bat.)

Brigade: GB Duppelin
25ème Ligne (3 Bat.)
85ème Ligne (3 Bat.)

Foot Battery (6 x 8pdr.)
Horse Battery (6 x 4pdr.)

**2ème GROSSE CAVALERIE DIVISION:
GD Saint Sulpice**

Brigade: GB Clément
1ère Cuirassiers (4 sqns)
5ème Cuirassiers (4 sqns)

Brigade: GB Guiton
10ème Cuirassiers (4 sqns)
11ème Cuirassiers (4 sqns)

Horse battery
(4 x 8pdr. and 2 x 6pdr. howitzers)

Unattached Division
**1ère GROSSE CAVALERIE DIVISION:
GD Nansouty**

Brigade: GB Defrance
1ère Carabiniers (4 sqns)
2ème Carabiniers 4 sqns)

Brigade: GB Doumerc
2ème Cuirassiers (4 sqns)
9ème Cuirassiers (4 sqns)

Brigade: GB Saint Germain
3ème Cuirassiers (4 sqns)
12ème Cuirassiers (4 sqns)
Horse battery
(4 x 8pdr. and 2 x 6pdr. howitzers)

IV CORPS
COMMANDER: MARÉCHAL MASSENA
Total strength approx. 26,100 infantry,
3,800 cavalry, 68 guns
(Massena's corps did not arrive in time to
take an active part in the battle.)

1ème DIVISION: GD Legrand

Brigade: GB Ledru
26ème Légère (3 Bat.)
18ème Ligne (3 Bat.)

Foot battery (6 x 6pdr. and 2 x howitzers)
Horse battery (4 x 6pdr. and 2 x howitzers)

Baden Brigade: GB Kister/GM Harrant
Leib-Infanterie-Regiment Großherzog Nr. 1
(2 Bat.)
Linien-Infanterie-Regiment Erbgroßherzog
Nr. 2 (2 Bat.)
Jägerbataillon von Lingg (1 Bat.)

Foot battery
(4 x 6pdr. and 2 x 7pdr. howitzers)
Half Horse battery
(2 x 6pdr. and 2 x 7pdr. howitzers)

2ème DIVISION: GD Carra Saint-Cyr

Brigade: GB Cosson
24ème Légère (3 Bat.)

Brigade: GB Dalesme
4ème Ligne (3 Bat.)
46ème Ligne (3 Bat.)
(Of these nine battalions, it is possible that
only seven took part in the march north.)

Foot battery (6 x 6pdr. and 2 x howitzers)
Horse battery (4 x 6pdr. and 2 x howitzers)

**Hessen-Darmstadt Brigade: GB
Schinner/GM Nagel**

Leib-Garde-Brigade
Leib-Garde-Regiment (2 Bat.)
Leib-Garde-Füsilier-Bataillon (1 Bat.)

Leib-Brigade
1. Leib-Füsilier-Bataillon (1 Bat.)

Foot battery (5 x 6pdr., 1 x 7pdr. howitzer)

FROM II CORPS
Attached to IV Corps

2ème DIVISION: GD Claparède

Brigade: GB Cöehorn
17ème Légère (1 Bat.)
21ème Légère (1 Bat.)
26ème Légère (1 Bat.)
28ème Légère (1 Bat.)
Tirailleurs du Pô (1 Bat.)
Tirailleurs corses (1 Bat.)

Brigade: GB Lesuire
27ème Ligne (1 Bat.)
39ème Ligne (1 Bat.)
59ème Ligne (1 Bat.)
69ème Ligne (1 Bat.)
76ème Ligne (1 Bat.)

Brigade: GB Ficatier
40ème Ligne (1 Bat.)
64ème Ligne (1 Bat.)
88ème Ligne (1 Bat.)
100ème Ligne (1 Bat.)
103ème Ligne (1 Bat.)

Foot battery (6 x 4pdr., 2 x 6pdr. howitzers)
It appears Claparède marched with 18
guns in total, so I assume the additional
10 guns were allocated from the cavalry
Division, which had two batteries and/or
II Corps' artillery reserve.

Detached from **Cavalerie Légère Brigade:
GB Colbert**
9ème Hussards (3 Sqns.)

**3ème GROSSE CAVALERIE DIVISION:
GD d'Espagne**

Brigade: GB Raynaud
4ème Cuirassier (4 sqns)
6ème Cuirassier (4 sqns)

Brigade: GB Fouler
7ème Cuirassier (4 sqns)
8ème Cuirassier (4 sqns)

Horse battery
(4 x 8pdr. and 2 x 6pdr. howitzers)

The village of Eggmühl. The village and its vital bridge over the Grosse Laaber were defended by the two weakened battalions of Peterwardein Grenzers. Determined to capture both without delay, Napoleon ordered the Württemberg light troops to the attack. (D. Wright)

Rogging. Within a short space of time the heights south of the Grosse Laaber were in French-Allied hands.

DAVOUT LAUNCHES HIS ATTACK

The inn and Schloss in Eggmühl. The Württembergers' first two attempts to storm the bridge were beaten off by the Grenzers but a third attack, spearheaded by the König Jäger, succeeded, breaking into the village and advancing right up the castle.

The sound of gunfire from Buchhausen had alerted everyone. Davout, who had remained in position all morning, was relieved that the Austrians had not opened an offensive against him. At about 2.00pm he set his men in motion. Initially Friant was to hold his position, but later he was to advance eastwards towards the Sanding villages. On his right St. Hilaire moved forward with Destabenrath's brigade on the left and Lorencez's on the right, aligned on Unterlaiching. Next came Deroy's Bavarian Division, which Lefebvre ordered to advance with its left on Unterlaiching, while the right, with Seydewitz's cavalry, were to aim for the hills behind the village. Demont's Division advanced along the northern bank of the Grosse Laaber towards Eggmühl, with one battalion on the southern side. Kronprinz Ludwig's Bavarian Division, which had marched up from Langquaid and arrived behind Schierling around midday, were to follow Deroy and Demont. St. Germain's Cuirassiers rode off to rejoin Nansouty with Napoleon's main cavalry force. Napoleon wasted no time in joining his forward troops, and from the hill at Lindach he observed the field of battle spread out before him. Across the valley of the Grosse Laaber he could see Davout's Corps moving forward. Therefore to increase the pressure on the Austrian left, Napoleon ordered the Württembergers to capture the bridge and village of Eggmühl, which would enable him to transfer his troops, particularly the cavalry, to the northern bank of the river. At the same time, Lannes was to move to the right with Gudin and Morand's Divisions, find a way across the river towards Rogging and advance against the extreme left of the Austrian line.

The sound of firing at Buchhausen had alerted Rosenberg to the coming danger too, and this was confirmed by Vuskassovich, as he fell back to Eggmühl. It was only a short time before his artillery opened up and added to the sound of the fire which was closing in on his position from front and left. Rosenberg sent news of the danger to Charles and then prepared to secure himself as best he could. To support Vukassovich, who was now at Eggmühl, Rosenberg ordered the two battalions of IR9 Czartoryski and the two batteries on the hill south-west of Unterlaiching to pull back onto the high ground behind that village. The infantry moved onto the Bettelberg, while the artillery occupied the

Vorberg, a flat hill projecting southwards from the Deisenberg, with a clear field of fire towards the Grosse Laaber. Formed up on the hills close to these batteries were Stutterheim's 4. Vincent-Chevauleger and 10. Stipsicz-Husaren. At about 3.00pm, with enough of his men now formed for an attack, Napoleon ordered his army forward. While Gudin's Division moved to the river and began to push across towards the heights above Rogging, the Württemberg light infantry moved against the Eggmühl bridge.

THE ATTACK ON EGGMÜHL

Defending this small but vital bridge were 1st Battalion, 9. Peterwardein Grenzer. The 2nd Battalion was behind, occupying the village and castle. Effectively utilising the cover provided by the trees

THE CAPTURE OF EGGMÜHL
Upon his arrival at Eggmühl, Napoleon determined to capture the village without delay. The task was handed to the Württemberg light infantry who, spearheaded by the König Jäger, forced the passage of the Grosse Laaber on the third attempt. Continuing their advance, they drove the Peterwardein Grenzer back and captured the village, allowing Napoleon to establish his men on the Austrian flank.

The Schloss at Eggmühl. On the right is the front elevation and entrance to the castle. The left-hand picture shows the older part of the castle at the rear. (D. Hollins)

growing along the river bank, the Grenzer, weakened by the actions at Bachl and Teugn-Hausen, opened a heavy and destructive fire against the Württemberg light battalions. With supporting artillery fire from the battery below the Bettelberg, the first two attempts to take the bridge failed, with heavy casualties, but with great courage a third attempt was made, spearheaded once again by the König Jäger, with a company of the von Neuffer Jäger and supported by their horse artillery. This attack came forward with such ferocity that it broke through the Grenzer line and its impetus carried it along the road as it curved to the right into the village itself. Although facing increased fire from the defenders of the castle, the attackers were able to continue right up to its walls, while the rest of the brigade followed up. Undaunted, the König Jäger then smashed through the door of the castle and engaged in hand-to-hand fighting with the defenders. At the same time, the 3rd Battalion of the 12ème Ligne from Gudin's Division which had crossed the river joined the attack. Isolated and outnumbered, the 300 remaining defenders surrendered. The exhausted Württembergers, pushed beyond endurance, sank down to rest. Behind them the bridge and streets of Eggmühl were strewn with the dead and dying of both sides. An eyewitness wrote: "There lay now many men and horses, smashed wagons, cannons, muskets, cartridge boxes, boots still containing feet, hands, arms and heads all around."

GUDIN CROSSES THE GROSSE LAABER

Gudin's Division had meanwhile discovered a way across the Grosse Laaber at Stangmühl, between Eggmühl and Rogging, and had engaged the skirmishers from Bieber's brigade. The exchange increased in intensity, and as more men became involved, the Austrians were forced to give ground and fell back to some woods close to the road, just to the north-east of Eggmühl. Here they were able to hold their position and repel all French attacks.

While the Württembergers were struggling for the possession of Eggmühl, Napoleon had been building up his cavalry south of the Grosse Laaber. Soon 53 squadrons were arrayed in two long lines waiting

The Schloss was defended by about 300 of the Grenzers. The König Jäger attacked the building and broke through the main door. With a battalion from Gudin's Division joining the attack, the Grenzers, now isolated, surrendered. (D. Wright)

for orders to cross. In addition von Seydewitz's squadrons north of the river were occupying the hill south-west of Unterlaiching which had recently been vacated by the Austrian guns. Against this massive mounted force, Rosenberg could muster only 19 squadrons. His appeals to Charles earlier in the day for four kürassiere regiments (24 squadrons) had met with no response.

Charles Decides to Avoid Battle

Charles was at Thalmassing. Here he had received Rosenberg's report of the approach of an enemy force from Landshut between 1.00 and 2.00pm. The reason for his opponents' apparent inactivity of the morning became crystal clear. Considering the position of his army, which was just beginning its advance, Charles felt that it was impossible to reinforce IV Korps to any great degree. To issue revised orders to the army, now on the move, reorganise the columns and realign on a new line of march across poor quality woodland tracks would take far too long. Also, being unaware of the strength of the Landshut column, Charles still believed that the French were in strength before him, so a march to the south by his army would in turn expose his right to attack. Charles decided that his only choice was to avoid battle, pull the army back and re-form it on the hills south of Regensburg. From there he could choose to stand and fight or retreat back over the Danube.

At about 2.00pm Charles wrote to Rosenberg, informing him of his decision and giving him the stark message to pull out of the battle as best he could. By the time Rosenberg received this order, his command, about 18,000 strong, was heavily involved right along its entire front with the converging French-Allied army, which could ultimately draw on over 90,000 men. Some time after 2.00pm orders were issued to the other commanders to halt their forward moves and march back to new positions in front of Regensburg. A message was also despatched to Bellegarde, whose I Korps were looking for an enemy that did not exist north of the Danube, to pull back to Regensburg.

Austrian IV Korps Become Rearguard of the Army

Once the village of Eggmühl had been secured, the cavalry funnelled

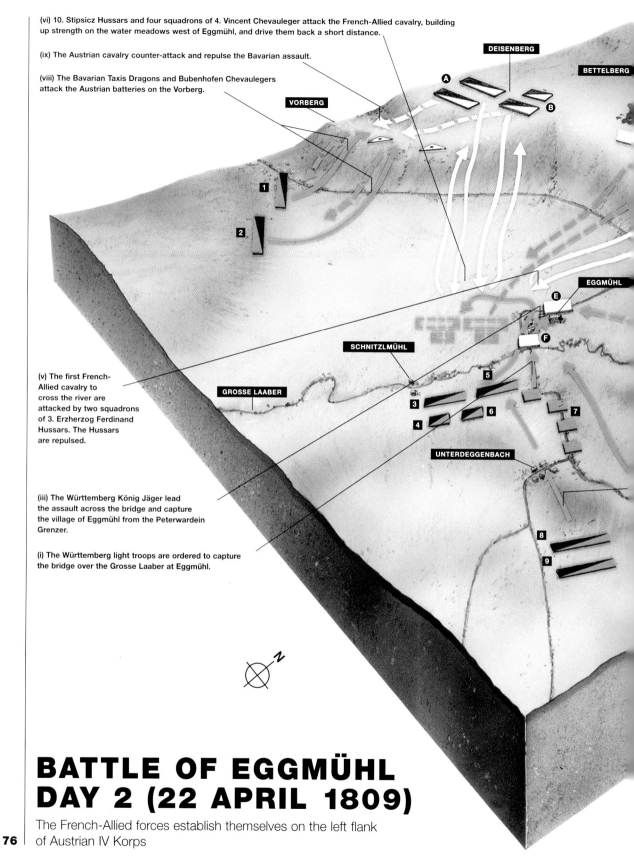

(vi) 10. Stipsicz Hussars and four squadrons of 4. Vincent Chevauleger attack the French-Allied cavalry, building up strength on the water meadows west of Eggmühl, and drive them back a short distance.

(ix) The Austrian cavalry counter-attack and repulse the Bavarian assault.

(viii) The Bavarian Taxis Dragons and Bubenhofen Chevaulegers attack the Austrian batteries on the Vorberg.

DEISENBERG

BETTELBERG

VORBERG

EGGMÜHL

SCHNITZLMÜHL

(v) The first French-Allied cavalry to cross the river are attacked by two squadrons of 3. Erzherzog Ferdinand Hussars. The Hussars are repulsed.

GROSSE LAABER

(iii) The Württemberg König Jäger lead the assault across the bridge and capture the village of Eggmühl from the Peterwardein Grenzer.

(i) The Württemberg light troops are ordered to capture the bridge over the Grosse Laaber at Eggmühl.

UNTERDEGGENBACH

BATTLE OF EGGMÜHL
DAY 2 (22 APRIL 1809)

The French-Allied forces establish themselves on the left flank of Austrian IV Korps

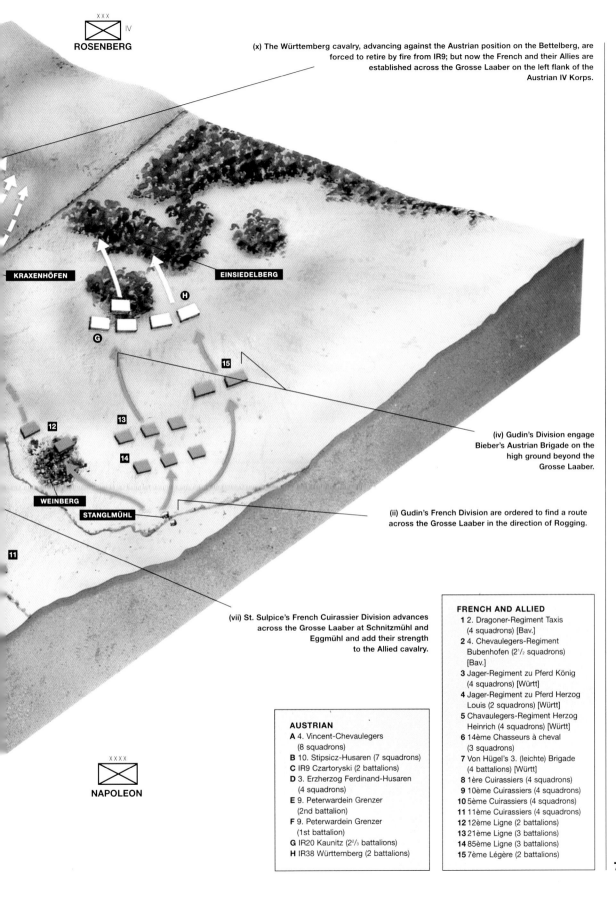

XXX
IV
ROSENBERG

(x) The Württemberg cavalry, advancing against the Austrian position on the Bettelberg, are forced to retire by fire from IR9; but now the French and their Allies are established across the Grosse Laaber on the left flank of the Austrian IV Korps.

KRAXENHÖFEN

EINSIEDELBERG

H

G

15

13

12

14

(iv) Gudin's Division engage Bieber's Austrian Brigade on the high ground beyond the Grosse Laaber.

WEINBERG

STANGLMÜHL

(ii) Gudin's French Division are ordered to find a route across the Grosse Laaber in the direction of Rogging.

11

(vii) St. Sulpice's French Cuirassier Division advances across the Grosse Laaber at Schnitzmühl and Eggmühl and add their strength to the Allied cavalry.

XXXX
NAPOLEON

AUSTRIAN
A 4. Vincent-Chevaulegers
(8 squadrons)
B 10. Stipsicz-Husaren (7 squadrons)
C IR9 Czartoryski (2 battalions)
D 3. Erzherzog Ferdinand-Husaren
(4 squadrons)
E 9. Peterwardein Grenzer
(2nd battalion)
F 9. Peterwardein Grenzer
(1st battalion)
G IR20 Kaunitz (2²/₃ battalions)
H IR38 Württemberg (2 battalions)

FRENCH AND ALLIED
1 2. Dragoner-Regiment Taxis
(4 squadrons) [Bav.]
2 4. Chevaulegers-Regiment
Bubenhofen (2¹/₂ squadrons)
[Bav.]
3 Jager-Regiment zu Pferd König
(4 squadrons) [Württ]
4 Jager-Regiment zu Pferd Herzog
Louis (2 squadrons) [Württ]
5 Chavaulegers-Regiment Herzog
Heinrich (4 squadrons) [Württ]
6 14ème Chasseurs à cheval
(3 squadrons)
7 Von Hügel's 3. (leichte) Brigade
(4 battalions) [Württ]
8 1ère Cuirassiers (4 squadrons)
9 10ème Cuirassiers (4 squadrons)
10 5ème Cuirassiers (4 squadrons)
11 11ème Cuirassiers (4 squadrons)
12 12ème Ligne (2 battalions)
13 21ème Ligne (3 battalions)
14 85ème Ligne (3 battalions)
15 7ème Légère (2 battalions)

77

across the bridge and through the village and began to redeploy on the water meadows on the north bank of the river. At the same time, other horsemen filtered across the river at two fordable positions west of the bridge that had been created by opening weir gates at Schnitzlmühl. But the ground was marshy, and this manoeuvre took some time to complete. The Austrian batteries on the Vorberg and Bettelberg were not slow to bring a heavy fire to bear on the horsemen. An attempt to disrupt this build-up was ordered by Stutterheim, who threw the 10. Stipsicz-Husaren and four squadrons of 4. Vincent-Chevauleger against the centre of the French-Allied line and succeeded in temporarily driving them back before returning to the heights.

The French Attack Unterlaiching

Meanwhile, the advance of St. Hilaire's Division had been gaining ground. Spearheaded by the 10ème Légère, the attack rolled forward against Unterlaiching and this time the village was taken fairly easily, since it had been only lightly defended. The majority of the two battalions of IR44 Bellegarde were defending the wood behind, where abattis of fallen trees had been constructed, but two companies were positioned in the walled cemetery on the extreme left of the village. However, once among the trees, they encountered a violent and ferocious resistance in the gloomy wood. To the right of IR44 the village and the area surrounding Oberlaiching was held by IR55 Reuss-Greitz. On the slopes to their right rear were IR46 Chasteler. The northern end of the line, including the woods, was held by 12. Deutsch-Banat Grenzer, IR8 Erzherzog Ludwig and IR22 Koburg.

As the French infantry moved forward they were supported by Deroy's Bavarians who were led by 14. Linien-Infanterie-Regiment. Seydewitz's cavalry, south-west of Unterlaiching, had also attracted unwelcome Austrian artillery fire. Having received permission to attack the guns on the Vorberg, Seydewitz began to advance. It appears that St. Sulpice was also ordered to attack, but he was either not yet in position

General Gudin, commander of the 3rd Division of Davout's corps. Now detached from III Corps and under Lannes' orders, with Morand, Gudin discovered a crossing point over the Grosse Laaber at Stangmühl towards Rogging. Gudin drove back Bieber's brigade to a wood north-east of Eggmühl.

Looking east towards the heights above Rogging. Eggmühl is hidden behind the trees on the left. In the right foreground is one of the many drainage channels that feed the Grosse Laaber. (D. Wright)

78

or failed to receive the order in time. The Bavarian cavalry crossed a small stream which ran south of Unterlaiching in dead ground, swung left into line and charged up the slope, 2. Taxis-Dragoner on the left, 4. Bubenhofen-Chevaulegers the right. Taken by surprise, the gunners managed to fire off one discharge of canister before the cheering horsemen were among them, swinging wildly with their swords. Five guns quickly fell into Bavarian hands, and just as success seemed certain, Stutterheim ordered four squadrons each from 4. Vincent-Chevaulegers and 10. Stipsicz-Husaren to counter-charge. The Austrian cavalry swept forward and crashed into the disordered Bavarians, pursuing them back down the hill. However, the pursuit was brought to a halt by a Bavarian battery on the hill south-west of Unterlaiching and musket fire from the infantry advancing against the village, drawn up in squares. Seydewitz's men re-formed among the main body of French-Allied cavalry. The Austrians re-formed on the Vorberg. At the same time, some Württemberg squadrons moved against the Bettelberg, but having driven off part of the Austrian cavalry there, they were repulsed by the fire of IR9 Czartoryski.

THE STRUGGLE FOR THE WOODS

The small hamlet of Kraxenhofen, just north of Eggmühl. The high ground directly behind is the Bettelberg. This high ground was occupied by two battalions of IR9 Czartoryski, half a regiment of cavalry, a cavalry battery and the Grenzers who had avoided capture in Eggmühl. (D. Wright)

Back in Unterlaiching the fighting was still rolling backwards and forwards through the wood. But as Deroy's Bavarians came up and began to outflank the position, the Austrians in the cemetery were captured and those in the wood forced to evacuate. IR55 had also been drawn into the fighting among the trees, but with their flank exposed and under increasing pressure to their front, they too fell back. French and Bavarian soldiers surged forward and dense swarms of skirmishers emerged from the wood in close pursuit. Stutterheim managed to halt IR44 and IR55. Quickly re-forming them, he drove their pursuers back and regained control of part of the wood. But the French 10ème Légère and Bavarian 14. Linien-Regiment fought back, retook the woods and

THE WOODS AT UNTERLAICHING

During the fighting on 22 April the French 10ème Légère captured Unterlaiching and continued their advance into the woods that clung to the hillside behind. The woods were resolutely defended by IR44 Bellegarde and it was only when infantry from the Bavarian 14. Linien-Infanterie-Regiment joined the attack that the Austrians were driven out.

advanced again. This time Stutterheim charged into them with four squadrons of 4. Vincent-Chevaulegers and drove them back once more. This charge enabled IR44 and IR55 to break off combat, and Rosenberg ordered them to march back to the Regensburg road. While this action had been going on, Bieber's brigade, IR20 Kaunitz and IR38 Württemburg, who had continued to defend resolutely against Gudin's Division, were finally unable to hold their position any longer and they also commenced falling back. Rosenberg was left with no choice but to order IR9 Czartoryski to retreat. This order was then issued to all other units of his korps. Bieber's brigade were kept well in hand during the retreat, and on a number of occasions halted and repelled French attempts to break into the column.

The units at the northern end of the IV Korps line had also been heavily involved in fighting. 12. Deutsch-Banat Grenzer in the wood between Oberlaiching and Obersanding had met the first French attacks led by 108ème Ligne supported by 111ème Ligne. The 33ème Ligne pressed towards Oberlaiching. The Grenzer were driven out and fell back towards Obersanding. In their place IR8 advanced into the woods to stem the French advance. Meanwhile, IR22 had moved to thwart an attempt to outflank the korps at Obersanding by parts of 48ème Ligne and 108ème Ligne. But by then events on the left of the korps at Unterlaiching had convinced Rosenberg that his position was no longer tenable. Having received their orders, they began to fall back through the Sandings towards Thalmassing, in good order.

The End of the Rearguard Action

The situation on the high ground behind Unterlaiching was now desperate: just the artillery and cavalry were left to prevent the infantry's retreat turning into a rout. The Bavarian cavalry launched a second charge against the guns on the hill, and again through a hail of canister they reached their goal, only to be counter-charged once more. Three squadrons of Stipsicz-Husaren and four of Vincent-Chevaulegers attacked and an indecisive mêlée flowed back and forth until

ABOVE **Kronprinz Ludwig with his staff on a hill north of Schierling. In the right background St. Hilaire's Division of III Corps can be seen moving towards Unterlaiching. (Bayerische Verwaltung, Munich)**

BELOW View from the Bettelberg. On the extreme left is the hamlet of Kraxenhofen, beyond which is Eggmühl. Extending away to the right of this village are the vast flat watermeadows where the French-Allied cavalry formed prior to attacking the Vorberg and Bettelberg. (D. Wright)

View from the Bettelberg. In the left background can be seen the church tower at Schierling. On the extreme right the hill with the pylon is the Vorberg; behind is part of the wood at Unterlaiching. It is up the slope of the Vorberg that Seydewitz's cavalry charged the Austrian guns.

Stutterheim charged in with the other four squadrons of the Vincent-Chevaulegers which had just recovered from driving the French and Bavarian infantry back into the wood. The Austrian cavalry pushed the Bavarians back through the guns, but now the Württemberg cavalry and French cuirassier were moving forward and had reached the top of the hill. The Württembergers charged into the flank of the great mêlée and turned the advantage back towards the German cavalry as the cuirassier crested the Bettelberg. Here Vukassovich's cavalry battery fired a parting blast of canister before rapidly limbering up and joining the exodus to the north. The remaining squadrons of Stipsicz-Husaren advanced into the overwhelming enemy force, but could only briefly halt its momentum. The valiant Austrian cavalry were beaten, and the two 12pdr batteries on the high ground were captured – they had performed heroics, and together they had gained much time and enabled IV Korps to extricate itself from a very exposed position.

It was now about 4.00pm. About this time Charles set out to ride back from Thalmassing to Alteglofsheim. However, he received news of the retreat of IV Korps. It would only be a matter of time before the pursuing enemy cavalry came into sight. Between 5.00 and 6.00pm Charles issued more urgent orders. Liechtenstein was to move his infantry with all speed to occupy a line between Gebelkofen and Köfering, while a kürassiere brigade were to take up a position on a low rise on the wide, open countryside south-east of Alteglofsheim.

Having secured Unterlaiching, St. Hilaire had swung his division to the north and followed Rosenberg's retreating korps towards the Sandings. As his leading skirmishers emerged from the twin villages, they were attacked and scattered by four hussar squadrons protecting the move towards Alteglofsheim. Some French hussars were also driven off, prompting St. Hilaire to halt his advance just north of Untersanding as the light began to fade. These four Austrian squadrons then observed the right of Friant's Division moving towards Thalmassing and attacked the lead skirmishers. The attack was not very successful, but it persuaded Friant's men against any further advance. Hohenzollern ran into the retreating IV Korps and grenadiers near Alteglofsheim, where he was forced to wait and let them pass before he could continue. Meanwhile, in the distance, French cavalry and artillery could be seen approaching from the south.

THE CAVALRY BATTLE AT ALTEGLOFSHEIM

Drawn up to face the might of the pursuing French army were the ten squadrons of Schneller's cavalry brigade, 1. Kaiser and 6. Gottesheim Kürassiere. Each regiment had detached a squadron at Thalmassing. To their right, on the slopes of the Rochusberg, was their supporting 6pdr. cavalry battery. As the tail of the Austrian army passed, moving northwards, the kürassiere were joined by Stutterheim and his light cavalry, who had fought so valiantly at Eggmühl. These exhausted men had gained some respite under cover of an artillery battery on the retreat, and they re-formed. Greatly weakened, they turned once more to make a stand with the heavy cavalrymen, bringing the total force to 29 squadrons. But as the French and Allied cavalry opposite them continued to grow, it became clear to the two commanders that there was little chance of victory, so the cavalry battery was sent to the rear, rather than risk losing it altogether.

THE CAVALRY CLASH AT EGGMÜHL

The Bavarian cavalry made two charges against a pair of 12pdr. batteries positioned on the Vorberg, behind Unterlaiching. On both occasions the Taxis-Dragoner and Bubenhofen-Chevaulegers were opposed by the Vincent-Chevaulegers and Stipsicz-Husaren. The first Bavarian attack was driven off, but while the second great mêlée was swirling around the guns, the Württemberg cavalry entered the fray and tipped the balance against the Austrians.

Under cover of their horse artillery, the French-Allied cavalry formed up. On the left, closest to the road, was Nansouty's Heavy Division, his three brigades deployed side by side with the carabiniers holding the centre. The two regiments in each brigade stood one in front of the other. Behind them St. Sulpice formed a second line with his four cuirassier regiments. To the right of the French came the Württemberg Jäger-Regiment zu Pferd König and two squadrons from Herzog Louis, along with three squadrons of the French 14ème Chasseurs à cheval. In reserve was Seydewitz's Bavarians and the 1. Chevaulegers-Regiment Kronprinz, who along with the Baden Leichte Dragoner-Regiment had been providing Napoleon's escort. In all, there were over 60 squadrons facing the Austrians as the weak April sun faded and twilight cast a sombre shroud over the gently rolling plain.

The light cavalry on the eastern flank were first to clash. The mêlée was inconclusive. Then, out of the gathering gloom, the white-coated Gottesheim Kürassiere advanced alone against the overwhelming mass

of Nansouty's heavy cavalry which was coming forward at a walk. As the kürassiere closed to a hundred paces, Nansouty's centre brigade, 1ème and 2ème Carabinier, halted and let off a volley from their carbines into the onrushing Austrians. Then the order was given to break into a trot.

Battle of Alteglofsheim. The heavily outnumbered Austrian cavalry made one more attempt to delay the pursuing French. The Austrian heavy cavalry charged into the French line with some initial success. but eventually they were driven from the field.

The two French brigades on the wings of Nansouty's Division were now ahead and had completely overlapped the Gottesheim line. Undeterred by the volley, the Austrians crashed into the carabinier with à force that echoed across the battlefield. The impact of their charge took some of the kürassiere through the first line of French cavalry, but as they came up against the second line, they could progress no further and the flanking French cuirassier were able to turn against the wings of the regiment. The situation was hopeless for the Gottesheim Kürassiere, but as the next Austrian attack rolled forward, they were able to extricate themselves and rode away northwards. This next attack was led by 1. Kaiser Kürassiere, supported by the Stipsicz-Husaren. The kürassiere crashed into the line, which prevented Nansouty following the first wave of defeated horsemen but failed to push them back any further. The hussars advanced into the mêlée, which now flowed around in a disordered tangle. 4. Vincent-Chevaulegers looked for an opportunity to hit the French at a vulnerable point, but as they moved forward, the Württemberg cavalry charged and threw them back. An attempt by 3. Erzherzog Ferdinand-Husaren was also defeated. It was all over and the outnumbered Austrians turned and ran.

The scene was one of great confusion as the horsemen fled back past Alteglofsheim towards Köfering. Archduke Charles himself was caught up in the disorder. Lederer's brigade of kürassiere was standing close to Köfering and 4. Kronprinz Ferdinand attempted to halt the victorious French cavalry but were themselves swept up in the retreat. All semblance of an orderly retreat came to an end as some of the Austrian infantry were ridden over by friend and foe alike. However, by now the French cavalry horses were completely blown, having ridden 45km that day, and the French were finally persuaded to end their pursuit by a few volleys from 3. Erzherzog Ferdinand-Husaren, east of Alteglofsheim, who seem to have retained some order. West of the town the pursuit was brought to a halt following a charge by two squadrons of 3. Herzog Albert-Kürassiere who were with Liechtenstein's column as it marched northwards.

BELOW **Battle of Alteglofsheim.** View from the Bochusberg to the north-east overlooking the vast open countryside where the great cavalry clash occurred on the evening of 22 April. (D. Wright)

CHARLES RETIRES
ACROSS THE DANUBE

The defeated Austrian army encamped uncomfortably on the hills and in the villages just to the south of Regensburg, individuals and groups striving to relocate the units from which they had become separated during the retreat. Charles rightly considered that his army was in no shape to form a new line the next day and fight again with the Danube at its back. He gave the order to commence a retirement through Regensburg to the north bank of the river during the night of 22/23 April. A pontoon bridge was constructed some 3,000 paces east of the great stone bridge. The Austrians continued to cross the river undisturbed, while five battalions from II Korps were detached to defend the city. Drawn up outside the walls was a rearguard of about 6,200 cavalry, which included Stutterheim's ubiquitous squadrons and a few infantry battalions. Napoleon and his exhausted army remained overnight on a line from Obersanding through Alteglofsheim.

As morning dawned, Napoleon prepared to retake Regensburg. Between 8.00 and 9.00am another series of great cavalry clashes began as the French horsemen – almost 10,000 strong – approached the city. In general the Austrian cavalry attacks were not well co-ordinated, with individual regiments throwing themselves against vastly superior masses of French horsemen, but the great bravery shown by these men against overwhelming odds succeeded in holding up the French advance for almost three hours, which gave the army enough time to retire across the Danube as well as the Regen at Rheinhausen. Their work done, the Austrian cavalry retired across the river. It was only at this point that the French became aware of the pontoon bridge but this was well defended and they were unable to capture it before the last Austrians withdrew and cut it loose.

Determined to carry Regensburg by storm, Napoleon now drew his army up before the walls and opened artillery fire. This barrage eventually created a breach in the wall and, after a number of fruitless attempts which brought heavy casualties, the French succeeded in entering the city. Meanwhile, groups of attackers had penetrated the defences at other points, and a vicious house-to-house battle through the burning city developed. Eventually the outnumbered defenders surrendered, but the French were unable to take the stone bridge since a battalion of IR15 Zach continued a ferocious defence of its northern gatehouse. It was about 9.00pm before the defenders abandoned this now ruined gateway to the northern suburb of Stadt-am-Hof.

THE STORM ABATES: CHARLES AND
HILLER WITHDRAW EASTWARDS

The first part of the campaign of 1809 was at an end. Archduke Charles' army, which had crossed into Bavaria on 10 April with great hopes of victory, was now, just two weeks later, split into two widely separated columns and retreating back towards Vienna. Yet although the battles of Abensberg and Eggmühl had ended Charles' offensive, neither wing of the army had been decisively beaten. Both were able to retreat intact; indeed Hiller's command were still able to turn and give their pursuers, led by Bessières, a bloody nose at Neumarkt on 24 April, the day after Regensburg was captured. Charles' wing of the army retreated through Bohemia unmolested as Davout, ordered to pursue him, kept his distance.

Napoleon was convinced that the two wings of the Austrian army would come together for a decisive battle before Vienna, around Passau, but he was wrong. Hiller's command engaged their pursuers once more,

ALTEGLOFSHEIM

On the plain to the south-east, the outnumbered Austrian cavalry make the last serious attempt to halt the French-Allied advance.

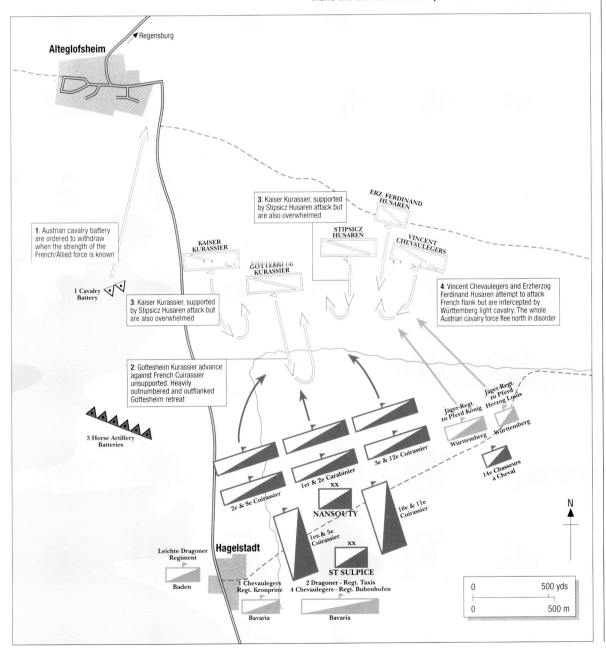

1: Austrian cavalry battery are ordered to withdraw when the strength of the French/Allied force is known

2: Gottesheim Kurassier advance against French Cuirassier unsupported. Heavily outnumbered and outflanked Gottesheim retreat

3: Kaiser Kurassier, supported by Stipsicz Husaren attack but are also overwhelmed

3: Kaiser Kurassier, supported by Stipsicz Husaren attack but are also overwhelmed

4: Vincent Chevaulegers and Erzherzog Ferdinand Husaren attempt to attack French flank but are intercepted by Württemberg light cavalry. The whole Austrian cavalry force flee north in disorder

at Ebelsberg on 3 May, before retreating again and finally crossing to the north bank of the Danube on 8 May. Shortly after, the two wings of the Austrian army were reunited and began to prepare for battle. Napoleon continued his march on Vienna, which was only lightly defended. The city surrendered after a bombardment on 13 May. The events of April had done little to improve Napoleon's impression of the Austrian army, but he had failed in his promise to annihilate it. In fact, at Eggmühl the greater part of his army had been delayed and prevented from coming to grips with Charles' main force by the resolute actions of FML Rosenberg, who had commanded what had become merely the rearguard of the Austrian army. Because of this failure, Napoleon's only

ABOVE **With the army safely across the Danube, Charles left a garrison of five battalions and artillery to defend the city. The city was bombarded and responsibility for its capture was handed to Lannes. After numerous failed attempts, the French finally broke in. (ASKB)**

concern now was to get across the Danube as fast as possible and catch up with the Austrians, who he believed were intent on retreating into Moravia as they had done in 1805. But Napoleon had underestimated his dogged opponents, for Charles was now planning a return to the offensive. And nine days after his capture of the empty prize of Vienna, Napoleon was to be handed his first taste of defeat at the ferocious and bloody battle of Aspern-Essling on 21–22 May 1809.

RIGHT **Once the French had entered the burning city, the fighting continued up and down the narrow streets and through the houses. Eventually the isolated garrison surrendered, but it was 9.00pm before the last Austrians defending the northern end of the Danube bridge were driven off. (ÖNB)**

91

THE BATTLEFIELDS TODAY

When planning a trip to the battlefields of the 1809 campaign in Bavaria, I think it best to allow yourself a minimum of three or four days to get a feel for the campaign. An excellent place to start is in Ingolstadt, at the Bavarian Army Museum. This really is a first-class museum, tracing the history of Bavarian soldiers from the 30 Years War to the present day, and includes a number of very interesting Napoleonic exhibits. From here, I suggest driving on to Regensburg. The city retains much of its history and is full of character. The old city walls are still in place, as are the gateways and the bridge across the Danube which neither side was able to destroy.

The battlefield of Teugn-Hausen lies less than 20km from the centre of Regensburg and is an easy drive. The area around the battlefield is farm and woodland. It is easy and enjoyable to explore it fully on foot as there are a number of convenient footpaths that run around and across the area between the Buchberg and the Hausener Berg and through the woods which saw some of the fiercest fighting.

The sprawling offensive of the Battle of Abensberg is not so easy to explore. Depending on which aspects of the battle you are most interested in, it might be best to devise your own route around this area. For a flavour of the country over which this running battle was fought, I suggest driving via Abensberg, through Bachl to Rohr, Rottenburg, Pfeffenhausen and on to Landshut. In the town there are plaques on

During the attempts to capture Regensburg, Napoleon was hit in the foot by a spent ball. The wound was minor, but the word went around that Napoleon was seriously hurt. To quell these rumours, he remounted his horse and rode where he could be clearly seen by his men. (P. Haythornthwaite)

Hiller again engaged his pursuers at Ebelsberg on 3 May. Much of the action centred on the 500-metre wooden bridge across the Traun river. The fighting through the streets and around the castle that followed was vicious and bloody. Hiller eventually pulled back and continued his retreat.

houses by the river commemorating the deaths of various officers in the second Battle of Landshut. The view across the river from the French side will seem familiar from early illustrations of the battle.

From Landshut the last leg of your journey will be along the Regensburg road, which will take you along Napoleon's route to Eggmühl itself. Here, all the prominent features of the battlefield are easy to find. The bridge over the Grosse Laaber (now a modern replacement) and the Schloss in the village should be visited. The Bettelberg and Vorberg and the woods behind Unterlaiching are all undisturbed, and as at Teugn-Hausen, footpaths extending across the area make it easy to explore.

For finding your way around the battlefields, I recommend the excellent maps in the Bavarian Topographische Karte 1:50000 series, while for footpaths and other finer details, their 1:25000 series is invaluable. Finally, the Bavarians are justifiably proud of their ancient brewing traditions, so do be polite and put a little time aside to sample the local brews!

WARGAMING EGGMÜHL

CAMPAIGN

Start the campaign from 10 April, when the Austrians first cross the border at the river Inn.

The French and allies:

Davout	III Corps	between Regensburg & Ingolstadt,
Lefebvre	VII Corps (Bavarian)	on the river Iser
Massena	IV Corps	Lech, south of Augsberg
Vandamme	VIII Corps (Württemburg)	Donauworth
Oudinot	II Corps	Lech, south of Augsberg

C-in-C Berthier, until Napoleon arrives at Donauworth 16 April.
Lannes, Bessieres, Marshals with no Corps, arrive Vohburg 19 April.

The Austrian army

Bellegarde	I Korps	north of Passau, leading
Kolowrat	II Korps	north of Passau, following
Hohenzollern	III Korps	Mulheim
Rosenberg	IV Korps	Scharding, leading
Louis	V Korps	Braunau, following
Liechtenstein	I Reserve Korps	Scharding, following
Hiller	VI Korps	Braunau, leading
Kienmayer	II Reserve Korps	East of river Inn, Ried

Archduke Charles is with V Korps.

You will need the 1:25,000 version of the tourist map described in 'The Battlefields Today'. Give each corps a distinctive marker scaled to four square kilometres for the umpire to move on the map. Each movement period represents six hours during which a corps can either sleep, eat, march 15km or fight. Each active period must be matched by a period resting within 24 hours or the troops become tired; drop one morale category, take a minus on firing and fighting and can no longer make charge moves.

Orders are delivered by couriers moving at 60 km per period. This may seem slow but they have to find their own way and the person to whom the message is addressed. This campaign suffered from considerable fog of war which is always difficult to reproduce in a game situation; all orders, reports etc. must be written on paper only 5cm square. The umpire should issue each player only enough to write to each of his marshals once per day on a campaign day basis. They can be saved up if not used but must only be issued at the above rate for the whole of the campaign. If lost and can't be read, too bad! When the players run out of order sheets they can either rush their personal figure around the table top or wring their hands and gnash their teeth.

This should be enough to get the opposing army corps into contact at which point you can open up the campaign to other players as corps commanders. These in turn get only enough order sheets to communicate with each of their divisional commanders once per day. This allowance includes reporting back to their C-in-C.

The key to handling the resulting wide variety of battles is to adjust the structure of the forces so each player has between six and sixteen tactical units to manoeuvre. So, if each side is fielding just one or two battalions the tactical unit would be the company. For bigger battles brigades become the tactical units and so on.

Assume that each corps has enough ammunition for just eight periods fighting, after which it must either surrender, withdraw or be resupplied by a wagon train arriving from the direction of Vienna or Paris.

Each corps would include an engineering train with a pontoon bridge big enough to span ordinary sized rivers in one period but you will need two such trains to span the Danube taking two periods.

At this stage you only need the two C-in-Cs and an umpire. The players write orders for each marshal and pass them to the umpire who calculates their arrival time and moves the corps markers on the map. He will report any news or contacts after making allowance for courier movement etc.

Recreating the historical battles should be much less taxing.

First Landshut is a classic delaying action. Set the terrain out as described in the text and deploy the Bavarians first. Using the scaled down equivalent of half a corps, the Austrians, of course, get five times as much, but how many will they be able to deploy? The Austrians arrive in column of march on the road from the south so will have to form up according to a pre-written order of battle during the game. Your rules will need a formula to convert playing time into real time. As the battle started at 10.00am the Bavarian troops will need to hold the Austrians up for one and a half campaign moves, nine hours before twilight starts to fall giving them just enough time to move out before complete darkness descends.

For Teugn-Hausen, use the bird's-eye view as the basis for your table and position the troops as described in the text. Most conventional rules will cope with this battle quite well, with 15mm figures organised into battalions, cavalry regiments and artillery batteries. The battle seems to have started around 9.00am giving ten hours of good daylight. It will be important also to represent the brigadier's figures on the table. Davout's redirection of Morand and Gudin's divisions make the fight a bit one-sided so their arrival should be diced for starting at noon. Roll a d6 for each unit arriving, that is the delay in hours before they arrive at the edge of the wood nearest the Austrians. The Austrian battle objective was to force Davout back towards the Danube where he could be caught in their pincer movement. In that context they have merely to hold the French forces in this battle before the rest of the pincer arrives to claim a strategic victory.

At Abensberg it is the Austrians who are trying to hold up the French. Set the table up to play down the long axis. At one end the table represents Rottenburg and sanctuary for the Austrians. The leading elements of the Bavarians deploy at the other end. A slightly meandering road connects the two. In between are, first, Thierry's command at

Offenstetten, then Schustekh with eight companies and four squadrons at Rohr. Plodding along the road connecting all these features are scattered elements of Austrian baggage train about to get in everyone's way. See if you can get any Austrians at all back to Rottenburg alive.

The Biburg-Pfeffenhausen retreat can be handled in the same way. Space the features out on the long axis of the table, the French at one end, Pfeffenhausen at the other. Deploy the various Austrian units in their forward positions and the French heads of columns just on the table edge. It is only a realistic option with 15mm or smaller figures. These make for unusual and challenging games, but the tables have to be short enough for French infantry to just reach the far end in one game day.

Second Landshut seems more appropriate in skirmish form, individuals fighting house to house. Make the streets narrow and the buildings around three storeys high, they are unlikely to have a basement. Make floor plans of each level and roll a d10 for the Austrians in each room, counting ten as zero. Effectively there is no limit to the French numbers. You could even try storming the bridge. Make it wide enough for eight figures abreast with Austrians manning the walls above the gatehouse and the windows of buildings either side. There could even be a light gun or two just inside the gatehouse to catch the first rush after the pioneers have done their work.

For Eggmühl, set the table up as the day one bird's-eye-view with the various battalions as shown. Note that the Austrians were using companies as tactical units at this stage. 1/300th-scale figures would be good for refighting this action, but 15mm figures will work too. If the French can force the Austrians off the table there is no need to refight the historical day two. On the other hand if the Austrians can emulate their forebears, recreating the day two battle will be a necessity.

Based on the day two bird's-eye-view, construct a table top along the axis of the action so you miss off the top and bottom corners of this view. In 15mm or 1/300th, you should be able to refight the whole action on the table top. In 25mm you get to fight three separate battles: the action around Eggmühl itself and each wing. For the Austrians to win they must hold on until Charles can transfer reinforcements to this part of the battlefield or launch an attack elsewhere to draw off the French/allied troops. As the French attack on Eggmühl started around 3.00pm the French have just four and a half hours to carry the position before nightfall, giving Charles the breathing space he needs.